The Rabbi's Cat

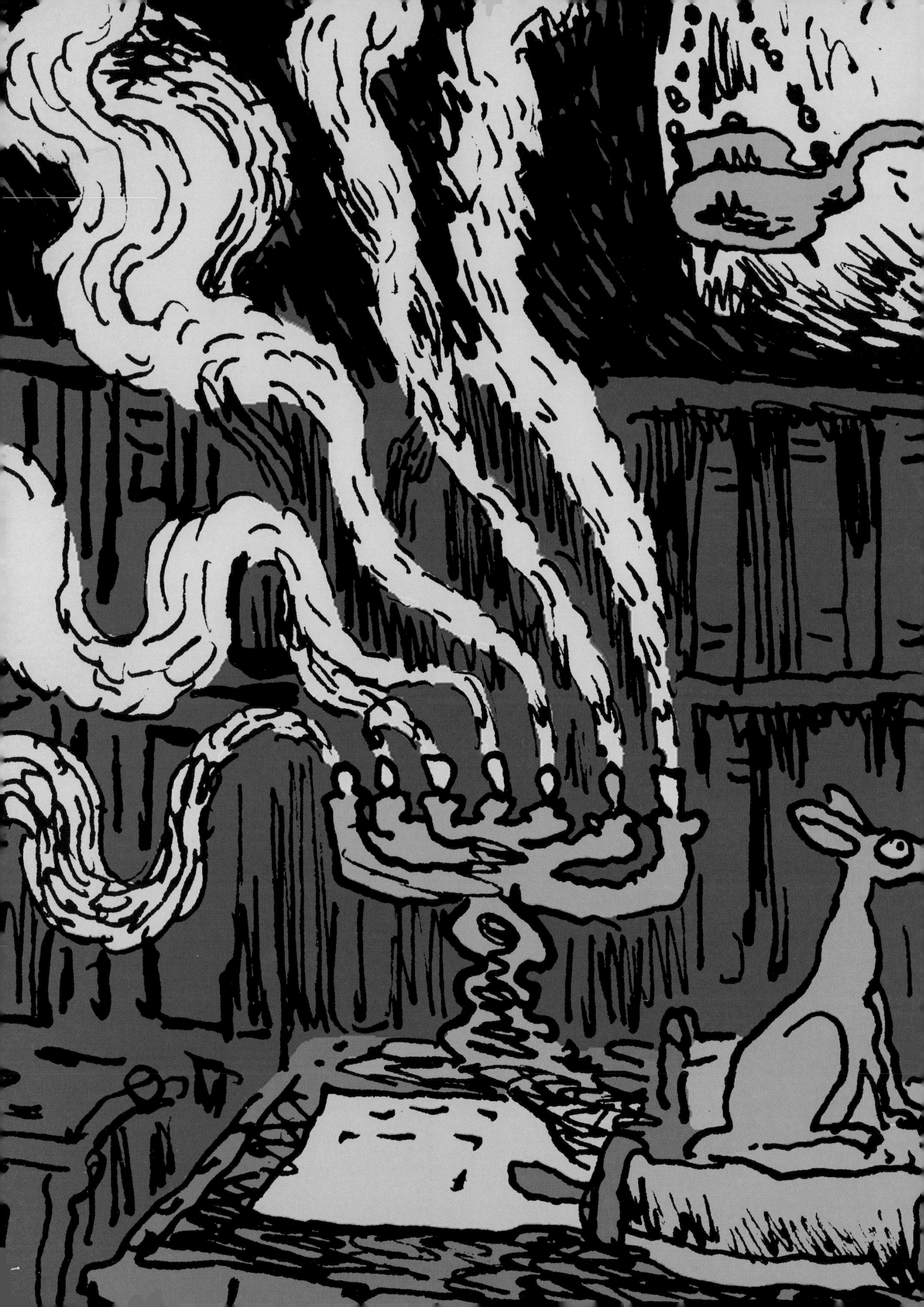

The Rabbi's Cat

JOANN SFAR

Color by Brigitte Findakly

Pantheon Books, New York

Library of Congress Cataloging-in-Publication Data
Sfar, Joann.
[Chat du rabbin. English]
The rabbi's cat / Joann Sfar.
p.   cm.
ISBN 978-0-375-71464-1
I. Title.

PN6747.S48C4813 2005
741.5'944—dc22
2004061406

www. pantheonbooks.com
Printed in Singapore
First American Paperback Edition
2 4 6 8 9 7 5 3

1.
THE BAR MITZVAH

I want to study the Kabbala, I tell him. No, he answers. You're ignorant. You don't understand a thing. You have to start at the beginning.

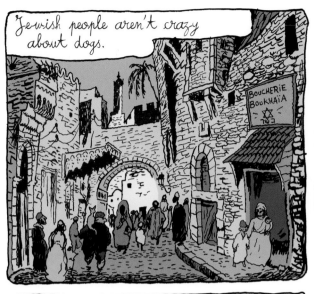

Jewish people aren't crazy about dogs.

A dog will bite you, chase you, bark.

And Jews have been bitten, chased, and barked at for so long that, in the end, they prefer cats.

Well, maybe not all Jews, but that's what my master says.

I am the rabbi's cat.

I don't disturb him when he reads.

The rabbi doesn't bother me either when I do things.

He says he has to respect my free will.

He also says that my freedom ends where the freedom of others begins.

But when he says that, I don't listen. I am absolutely free.

The only thing that could curb my complete freedom would be if someone slapped me around.

But the rabbi says that the human hand is too subtle a tool to hit people or cats with.

In the rabbi's house, there is a parrot.

I don't like him because he's noisy.

CAW!

I never speak.

CAW! CAW! CAW!

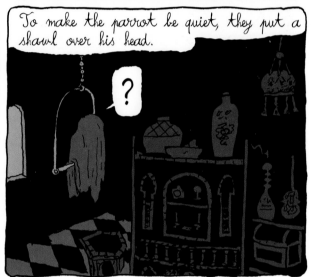

To make the parrot be quiet, they put a shawl over his head.

?

Then he thinks it's nighttime. And he sleeps.

ZZZ...

At night I don't sleep.

3

There is also my mistress, Zlabya.

She is the rabbi's daughter. Her name sounds like a honey-drenched pastry.

CLING! CLONG!

She takes good care of me, because she doesn't go out much.

RRRRRR

I go out every night.

I have adventures. My mistress doesn't know anything about this.

4

My mistress, Zlabya, says that if cats could talk, they would tell incredible stories.

She also says that if the parrot could shut up from time to time, it would give us a break.

The riches of the world should be better shared, she says.

This bird who has nothing to say talks endlessly.

While this cat, who roams the rooftops every night, never pipes up.

The rabbi tells her it's better this way.

5

I can't talk, but I know how to listen.

When my mistress pets me, I listen to her for hours.

I give her deep looks to tell her that I understand her.

Sometimes I close my eyes to show that with her I feel safe.

The parrot...

CAW!
CAW!
CAW!
CAW!
CAW!
CAW!

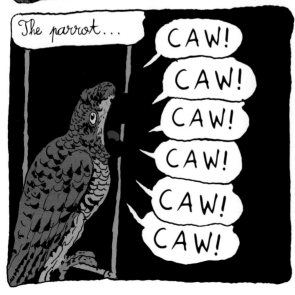

...gets tiresome.

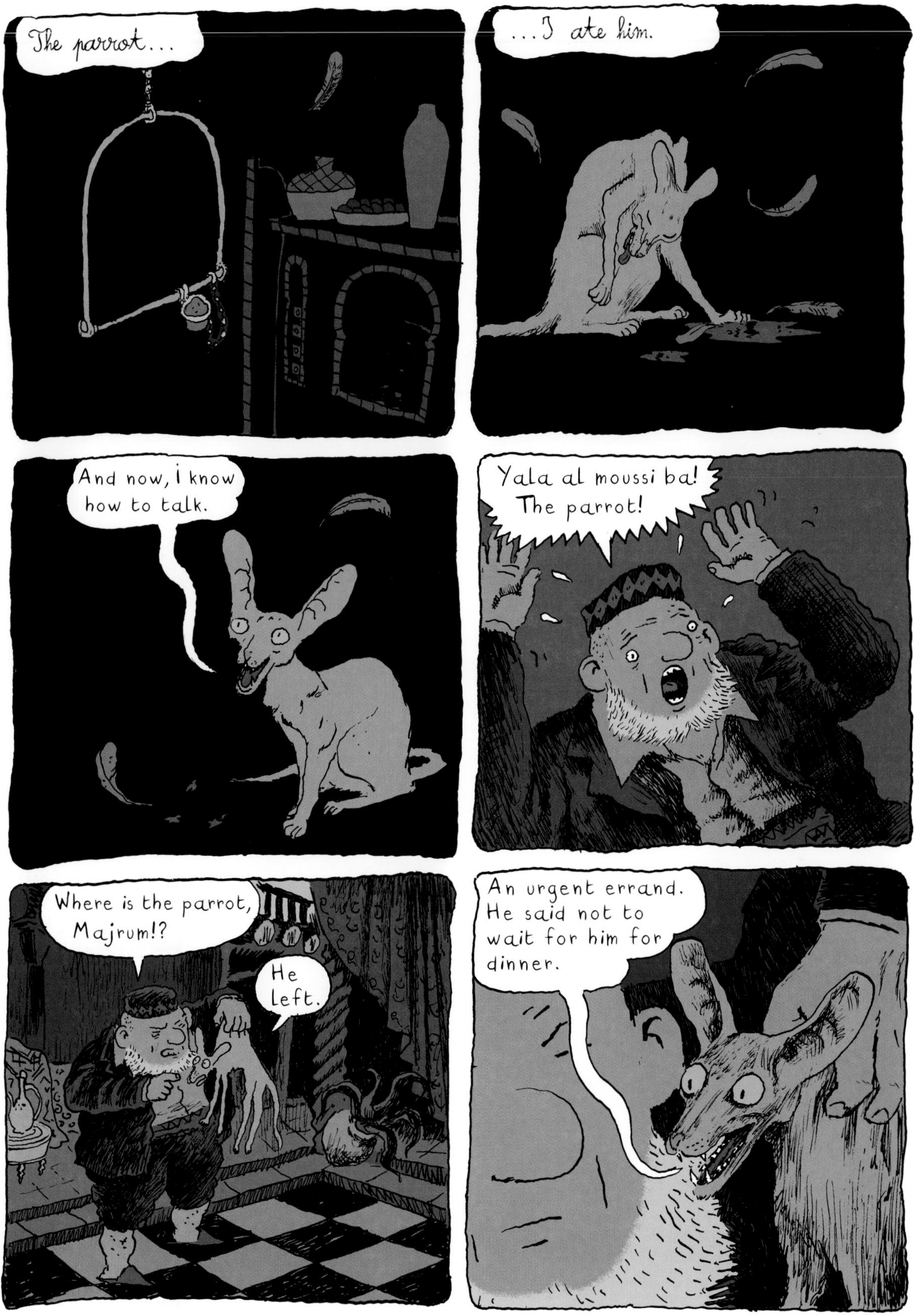

The parrot...
...I ate him.
And now, I know how to talk.
Yala al moussi ba! The parrot!
Where is the parrot, Majrum!?
He left.
An urgent errand. He said not to wait for him for dinner.

Zlabya, my daughter, a miracle has happened! The cat can speak!

Oh, Father, that's wonderful!

Yes, but there's a great misfortune too.

What is it?

He tells only lies.

That's not true!

Is it my fault if the parrot decided to split? What can I tell you?

The truth. The word exists to speak the world, not falsify it, Shaitan!

Maybe, but I didn't eat any parrot.

And these feathers in your mouth? Ah! Cain! You lie. You lie!

And even if he does tell lies, Father, is it really so bad?

It's terrible, my daughter.

8

The rabbi no longer wants me to be alone with my mistress.

He is afraid that I will put bad ideas into her head.

So he keeps me with him.

He wants me to study the Torah, and the Talmud—the Mishnah, the Gemara. He wants to put me back on the straight and narrow.

He tells me that I have to be a good Jew, and that a good Jew does not lie. I answer that I am only a cat.

I add that I don't know if I'm a Jewish cat or not.

9

The rabbi tells me that of course I'm Jewish, since my masters are Jews.

I tell him that I'm not circumcised.

He tells me that they don't circumcise cats.

I tell him that I haven't had a Bar Mitzvah.

He tells me that the Bar Mitzvah occurs at thirteen years of age. So I tell him that I am seven years old, and for cats, the years are multiplied by seven; therefore, it's as if I were seven times seven years old, which is definitely more than thirteen.

I tell him that if I am a Jewish cat, I want to be bar-mitzvahed.

10

We go to the rabbi's rabbi to ask him if a cat that talks can be bar-mitzvahed.

The rabbi's rabbi says no, that Bar Mitzvahs aren't for cats.

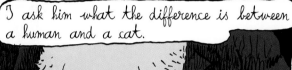

I ask him what the difference is between a human and a cat.

He replies that God made man in his own image.

I ask him to show me a picture of God.

He tells me that God is a word.

I say to the rabbi's rabbi that if man resembles God because he knows how to talk, then I resemble man.

He says no. Because my speech is evil. Because I acquired it in an act of killing.

I tell him that isn't true, that I didn't eat the parrot.

He says that, even worse, I am a liar.

I say that with speech, you can say what you want, even things that aren't true, that it's an amazing power, that he should try it.

The rabbi's rabbi tells the rabbi that he doesn't want to see me anymore and that I should be drowned.

The rabbi tells his rabbi that he won't drown me because he loves me and I don't like water.

And I tell the rabbi's rabbi that I am God, who has taken the appearance of a cat in order to test him.

I tell him that I am not at all satisfied with his behavior.

I tell him that he was as dogmatic and obtuse with me as some Christians are with Jews.

He gets on his knees and begs my forgiveness.

I tell him that it was a joke, that I'm only a cat, and that he can get up.

The rabbi's rabbi says that I blaspheme and that I lie and that I usurp the name of God and that I should be drowned.

The rabbi asks him if a rabbi shouldn't systematically accept contradiction from his students, if that isn't the very basis of Talmudic teaching.

Contradiction, yes, malice and malevolence, no, replies the rabbi's rabbi.

Students should bite their master the way puppies do.

In Jewish tradition, the dog is a good animal, says the rabbi's rabbi, because it is honest, persistent, and prepared to suffer for the common good. As for cats, pff! You can't trust a cat.

Blah blah blah! Nonsense! A dog is a sunny, simpleminded, moralistic, macho shit-head!

I ask the rabbi's rabbi where in the Bible he found this praise of dogs. He doesn't know.

I'm nocturnal, unpredictable, and deeply ethical.

He answers by talking about the oral Torah that wasn't fully written down.

He speaks of the spirit of the Law rather than the letter.

And then he tells me that the Greeks believed the dog to be the epitome of the philosophical animal. The dog, not the cat.

I reply that the Greeks destroyed the Temple of Jerusalem and if a rabbi ends up calling on them for help, it means he's run out of arguments.

He tells me that the Torah speaks more of humans than of dogs or cats, and that the question I've raised is pointless.

I tell him that's enough. That I want to have a Bar Mitzvah.

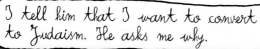
I tell him that I want to convert to Judaism. He asks me why.

I tell him that if I am a good Jew, the rabbi will let me spend time with his daughter.

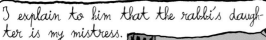
I explain to him that the rabbi's daughter is my mistress.

That I can't live without her, because she is my joy, and love is a beautiful thing.

He tells me that my motives for converting to Judaism are unsatisfactory, that my love of God isn't sincere.

I never said anything about love of God.

He explains to me that to become Jewish, you have to fear God and put yourself under his protection and cherish him.

He says that a Jew must see in all things the presence of God.

He says that thinking of God fills even the grayest days with sunlight.

He says that the love of God must be almost carnal.

He tells me that it is an intellectual love but you should always feel as though you were cradled in the arms of a master who is invincible, benevolent, and just.

I tell him that this is exactly what I feel for my mistress.

He tells me that since I am an animal who walks close to the ground on all fours, I can't raise myself up to the love of God.

He says that I can only limit myself to secular and imperfect loves.

I answer that he blasphemes, that my mistress is true.

He says that only God is true.

I say that God is a reassuring myth. I say that he doesn't have anyone to take care of him because he is old and his parents are dead.

I say that I have my mistress and I will never be alone because I will die before she does. He throws my master and me out.

Get out!

So we end up on the street, my master and I. And I can tell that my master's a bit angry with me.

Are you mad at me?

He's your master and you love him and I just proved to you that he's not all-knowing.

You're even realizing that, for all the deference you feel for him, this master is less intelligent than you are.

So you have no master, but you don't want to admit that, do you, because you don't want to end up old and alone and without anyone to turn to when you don't understand anything.

So you're going to do all you can to make the old man look good. And the more foolishness he talks, the more you'll call him "my master, my master, my master", as if to convince yourself.

Why are you so harsh?

I'm just trying to tell the truth, to see how it feels.

19

My master thinks I'm a bad animal, that I lie when I shouldn't and tell the truth only when it's hurtful.

I tell him that I've been hurting, too, ever since I started talking.

I tell him that I gained a power that I'd gladly do without, because when I was mute, I could spend days getting petted. I tell him that I'd do anything to see my mistress again. I add "Meow!"

Meow! Meow! Meow! I don't talk anymore, I meow, I pretend I'm still a normal cat.

But he tells me to stop. He says it's obvious I'm faking.

He says once you've left the Garden of Eden, you can't go back.

20

I tell my master that if his rabbi does not want to bar mitzvah me, we'll have to find another rabbi.

He tells me no sane rabbi will agree to instruct a cat in the precepts of the Law.

I tell him we could just find a rabbi who's crazy. He says he doesn't know any.

I tell him that if he loves me, he should be the one instructing me in the precepts of Mosaic Law.

You should teach me the Torah and then you can decide whether or not I'm qualified to have a Bar Mitzvah.

It's a very heavy responsibility. No, I can't.

But the rabbi's daughter cries because she no longer has her cat.

So the rabbi, who doesn't like to see his daughter cry, takes me on his lap to give me my first lesson in Judaism.

Pat! Pat!

21

"I want to study the Kabbalah," I say to him. "No," he answers. "You're ignorant. You don't understand a thing. You have to start at the beginning."

"I want to study the Kabbalah."
"No, you have to be at least fifty years old to study it, and you're only seven years old."

"Seven times seven is forty-nine," I tell him. "Forty-nine isn't fifty," he replies.

Get down here, and don't be such a mule.

"It's not true that you have to be old for the Kabbalah. That's just a trick of Talmud scholars to avoid competition from mystical doctrine," I say.

How do you know that?

I read it.

How long have you known how to read?

I always have. I learned at the same time as your daughter, but you didn't know before because I was mute. Teach me the Kabbalah.

Why the Kabbalah?

Because I like starting at the end.

No. With me, you learn things in order. You'll do as I say.

OK.

So we start at the beginning and my master teaches me that the world was created by God in seven days, five thousand seven hundred and some odd years ago.

I ask him whether he's pulling my leg. He says he's not, that it's the truth.

I tell him that's ridiculous and that with carbon-14 you can prove scientifically that the world has existed for billions of years.

Knock! Knock!

He tells me that carbon-14 can be wrong. That maybe the flood in Noah's time washed out the surface of the planet and made it seem like it was older.

I answer him that even a kitten would not buy this nonsense. He says that's what his master taught him. I tell him what I think of his master.

He tells me that maybe years only make sense if humans are there to count them. That maybe five thousand seven hundred years is actually the date of the first calendar. I like this explanation much better.

23

He tells me that Adam and Eve were the first humans. I ask him if Adam and Eve are a symbol.

He tells me that no, that's the actual truth. That they are the father and mother of us all.

I tell him that's a nice thought, that all humankind is one big family, but all the same, it's just a symbol.

He tells me that among Jews there are no symbols and no allegories.

He tells me Jewish teaching works by analogy.

He tells me I'm refusing to enter into it because my sight is clouded by Western thought.

24

"Western thought is a prehensile, predatory, and in the final analysis destructive machine, my master explains.

"It puts names to things, labels, as if to say "These things are part of my system, I have understood them."

But by the time you've finished naming a thing, it has already changed and the name you gave it no longer defines it exactly, so you end up with empty words in your mouth.

"Westerners want to resolve the world. Turn multiplicity into oneness. That's a delusion, says the rabbi.

But, master, doesn't Judaism also try to turn multiplicity into oneness?

Yes. But not in the same way.

Scratch!

Western thought works by thesis, antithesis, synthesis, while Judaism goes thesis, antithesis, antithesis, antithesis....

Slurp! Slurp!

25

I feel a bit guilty and I have to tell the rabbi.

The other day, when I let the rabbi's rabbi make a fool of himself because he couldn't come up with a biblical quote favorable to dogs, I was sneaky.

Because I know a passage in the Bible that praises dogs. Exodus 11:7, says "not a dog shall snarl..."

This "not a dog shall snarl" makes the dog a supporter of the Hebrews' liberation from Egypt.

The rabbi is impressed that I know so many things.

He says I am indeed guilty of having hidden my knowledge when it didn't suit my purposes.

But he also has a strange expression on his face. He tells me that he, too, has something to confess.

He admits that while his master was looking for a passage in favor of dogs, he thought of Exodus 22:31.

"You shall be holy people to me; you must not eat flesh torn by beasts in the field; you shall cast it to the dogs."

This passage likens the dog to a savage element that humanity must move away from, says the rabbi. It's a passage against dogs.

i could have quoted this passage to prove my master wrong and help you out, cat. But i, too, deliberately concealed my knowledge.

i did not want to contradict my master. i am as guilty as you are.

27

Before, when I couldn't speak, I had only simple dreams.

In my dreams I chased small animals.

Sometimes I managed to catch them and eat them.

Bigger animals chased me. I'd run very fast to escape from them.

At last, I'd find shelter in the arms of my mistress. She would pet me for hours to comfort me.

Giving me those sweet, gentle caresses that only women can give. Then I'd fall asleep. A young cat's dreams.

Since I've been able to speak, everything's changed. I have nightmares.

I dream that my mistress is ill and no one can cure her.

I dream that one day I don't see her anymore and I'm told that she's gone on a trip.

And I spend dream years telling everyone that she's away on a trip but is thinking about me. That she's coming back.

I wonder what kind of gift she'll bring back for me.

And one day, it pains the rabbi too much to hear me repeating that my mistress is traveling. He takes me onto his lap and tells me the truth.

She is dead.

29

Now that I can talk, I often dream that my mistress is dead, that the rabbi is alone with me.

Then the rabbi rejects religion. He no longer wants anything to do with a God who took his only child from him. He no longer believes in him.

While I, who never believed in God, have to pretend I do. To keep his spirits up.

We have to believe in an adult's God, I tell him, a veiled God who calls out to us by emptiness, by his absence.

We have to detect in reality the inner presence of God.

You have learned a lot, says the rabbi, but don't give me that garbage, I know it only too well.

And in my dream the rabbi no longer wants to study the Torah, or even to teach it. He renounces his master and dismisses his students.

So I tell him that I want to have my Bar Mitzvah, to motivate him so that he'll feel responsible for someone.

What will be the point, he asks, now that your mistress, my only daughter, is gone?

Exactly. It'll make me think of her. It'll be an homage.

My master replies that I know as much as he does, and that he doesn't know anything anyway. Enough with all this, he says.

And he adds that he can't understand why I want to be human when he would so much like to be a cat.

31

So, in this dream, my master and I turn into cats.

We roam the streets late at night.

We rummage through the garbage of non-kosher butchers.

Dogs chase after us but they don't catch us.

There are female cats that meow. I grab one by the neck and teach her a thing or two.

My master doesn't want to, not like that. Perhaps some remnant of his humanity, or Judaism, or just that he's old.

No, no, miss.

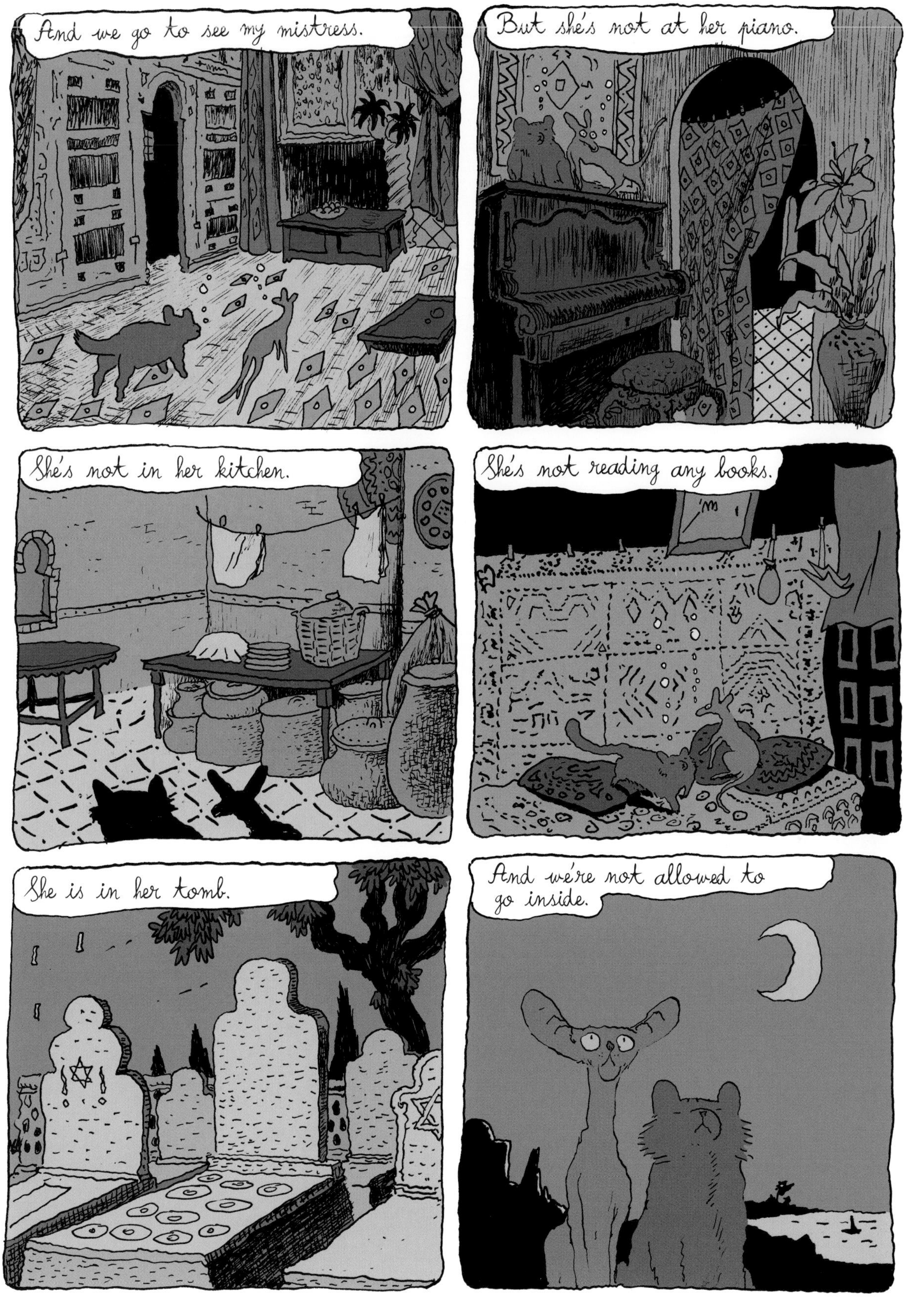
And we go to see my mistress.
But she's not at her piano.
She's not in her kitchen.
She's not reading any books.
She is in her tomb.
And we're not allowed to go inside.

My master wakes up in a sweat. He says he had a nightmare.

I say me too and ask him to tell me his nightmare.

I say that maybe we had the same dream.

But he doesn't want to talk about it. He says his morning prayers.

He says he preferred it when I didn't speak.

I say, me too—but it can't be helped.

My master goes to check whether Zlabya is all right.

She's fine, but we startled her out of sleep.

My master says, "I'm giving you back the cat, you're allowed to have him."

She asks, "Did he pass his Bar Mitzvah exam?"

The rabbi says this Bar Mitzvah business was nonsense.

"You're allowed to keep the cat, but he mustn't speak to you anymore."

I do as my master ordered.

RRRRRRR!

I behave like before, like a real cat.

My mistress knows that I understand her, that I can talk.

But she knows that I'll never speak to her again.

That's the deal, if I want to stay with her.

It's worth shutting your mouth to be happy.

This guy kicks me when the rabbi has his back turned.

I don't really like young men. Especially when they're passionate about religion.

hisss!

They wield it as an instrument of power.

Let's eat.

Scholarship allows them to speak at the table.

To get women's attention, to crush their rivals, to interrupt their father.

Such animals.

Tsss...

My master forbids me to show his disciples that I know how to talk.

...if the Jews have been massacred and persecuted, it's because that was God's will.

Jerk.

He also forbids me from telling him what I hear them say when he has his back turned.

If someone kills you, it's because you've been a bad Jew. If you move away from religion, you get punished.

Jerk.

And he even forbids me to bad-mouth them.

If you fear Hakadosh Baruch Hu, if you fear God, if you keep the Sabbath and say your prayers, nothing bad can happen to you.

It's obvious.

Jerk

If you practice Lashon Hara, speaking disparagingly of others, that is as serious as murder.

But all the same, master, I have to tell you. Your disciple Pinchas is the worst....

No. Don't say a word.

The commandment "Thou shalt not kill" counts malicious gossip as a blood crime.

So?

There's this one who is always ogling women on the sly, all sweatily.

He passes them on the street, keeping his neck stiff.

And once they've passed, he rolls his eyes and watches from under his arm.

When he gets to my master's house, he tells us that these women are lost.

That they should be forced to read The Guide for the Perplexed by Maimonides.

And my master smiles.

39

This guy adds that you could forgive non-Jewish women for showing their wrists and shoulders because they haven't received the Torah.

?

Speak, but be seated.

Therefore they don't know what makes the purity of a home. You can't blame those who are ignorant of the Law.

But with Jewish women who fall prey to these fashions worthy of the Amalekites, we should be pitiless, he says.

Why?

Yeah, why?

Other women have decided to show everything. But a Jewish woman guarantees the purity of her home.

Tsss...

Her table is a temple and she is its architect. She must save herself for her husband.

Have some more berbouche, no need to leave any.

If it's with that kind of talk that he hopes to marry the rabbi's daughter, he's got another thing coming.

One day I asked my master whether he thought his disciples masturbated.

He said certainly not; wasting the seed of life is an abomination.

I told him I couldn't agree more. "When I feel like fucking, I just fuck, but since the disciples are meant to be virgins until marriage and their testicles fill up every day, I don't know how they manage."

"They don't need to manage anything," my master answers. "They're not like you; they're not animals, but good Jews." That cracks me up.

My master is miffed, and he explains that humans can transform their sexual urges into energy that they use to learn and to enlighten their souls.

I'm sure that's true on some days, but I'll bet on other days they still jack off. But I don't dare say that to my master.

Sometimes I follow my master's young disciples down the streets. Nobody notices me. I'm just a cat, one of thousands.

I figure that when nobody's looking they must go to prostitutes or something like that.

Most of the time I'm disappointed that's not where they go. They go to the place of study, the yeshiva.

Or they go to the synagogue, or the Randon market.

Or they sit in the shade of a tree, drink tea, and talk about edifying subjects.

I'm disappointed that there isn't even one who goes to see prostitutes in secret. That upsets my theories.

42

I'm disappointed. Maybe my master is right. Maybe humans really are different from animals. Maybe they are able to "sublimate their libido," like he says.

Oh, here's the one I don't like. The braggart who doesn't know a thing but thinks he does and talks loudly and interrupts people and wants to marry my mistress. The young guy.

Where's he going? I'd like it if he went to the whorehouse.

He's going! He's going... no, he turned right, the whorehouse is to the left.

To the right is the Arab quarter. What's he doing there? Does he want his head to land up on the end of a stick?

But where is he going? If he had an Arab friend, or an Arab girlfriend, I'd find him a lot more endearing; but I don't believe it for a second.

43

I've got it!

He's going to the whorehouse for Arabs!

He figures that here at least no one will see him go in.

Hee! Hee! But I saw you, the guy who kicks me.

And I'm not allowed to say anything.

What torture!

44

I could go check out which girl he chose.

I could spy on him, see how he fucks.

Listen to hear whether he talks dirty during the act, that vindictive little saint.

I don't do it.

And it's not out of propriety.

It's painful to admit, but I think I feel some compassion for the boy.

Ever since I learned to speak, I've really turned into quite a funny creature.

Here I am feeling sympathy for a human who kicks me.

As long as I thought him unyield-ing and virtuous, I hated him.

Now that I know him to be two-faced and hypocritical, now that I've seen him struggle between his hor-mones and his beliefs, I love him.

Come to me, my little perplexed soul!

purr purr purr

BONK!

2.

MALKA OF THE LIONS

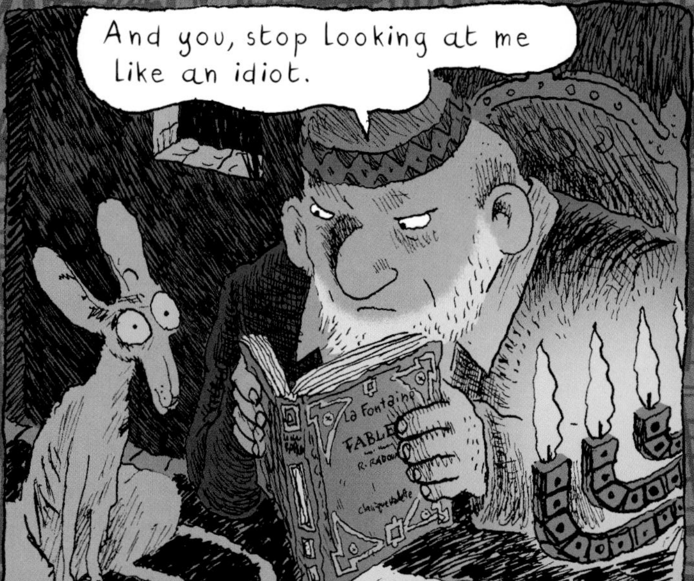
And you, stop looking at me like an idiot.

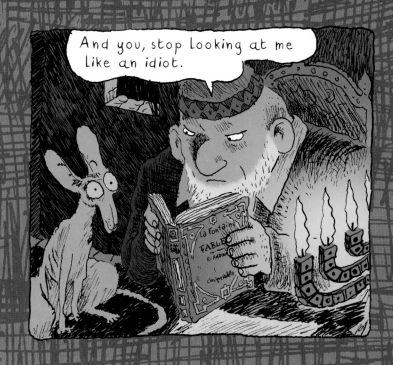

My master received two letters this morning. He doesn't open them right away. He starts with his morning prayer.

Then he has his breakfast.

One of the letters comes from Paris. The other is so beat up it looks as though it has crossed the desert.

Zlabya, my mistress, is curious to know what's in the letters, and so am I because cats are even more curious than girls are.

SLURP

The rabbi puts the letters in his pocket and goes out. He says he'll read them later.

Actually, I think he's drawing out the pleasure. Zlabya doesn't dare run after him. But I do.

The rabbi must want to settle down comfortably in the sun before reading his mail.

The terrace of Café L'Univers, run by the Carbodel family, offers an ideally sunny spot. We don't usually come to this café.

My master sits down at the best table, places his letters in front of him, and wonders what to order.

A waiter points out to us that the establishment serves neither Arabs nor Jews.

My master humbly asserts that this is not mentioned anywhere. The waiter tells us to beat it.

My master apologizes and we go read the mail elsewhere.

My master sits down next to a fountain. At least the sun belongs to everyone, he says. And here we have water, which is the best drink of all.

I would've preferred a bowl of milk. Anyway, we open the mail.

A Jew arrives.

Ah, rabbi, you caught me at a perfect time!

I'm the one being caught, Birkat Hacohanim. How is your wife?

The rabbi gets up to greet him, holding the letters behind his back. I can't wait for him to go.

She's fine, thank God; she screams all the time, which means she's in good health. I hope my daughters won't turn out the same way, because to marry them, M'ksina, I'd need help from God and the prophets, not to mention deaf husbands. Rabbi, I have a question.

Ask your question, Birkat Hacohanim.

He doesn't leave. He asks for the rabbi's advice on a particular point of the Law that's been bugging him.

My question is this. Ashkenazim wait five hours before drinking milk after eating meat, while we Sephardim wait only three hours. Imagine, God forbid, that I had to eat with one of these Jews from the cold and I felt like having milk four hours after the beef stew or God knows what meat they serve in that Poland of theirs.

Yes, so what?

Yikes! At least at the Carbodel café we'd have been spared this one.

Well, would I have the right to drink milk as a Sephardic Jew, or would I have to conform to this polar Jew's ways out of respect for him?

Do you know any Ashkenazim, Birkat Hacohanim?

No.

So why do you ask the question?

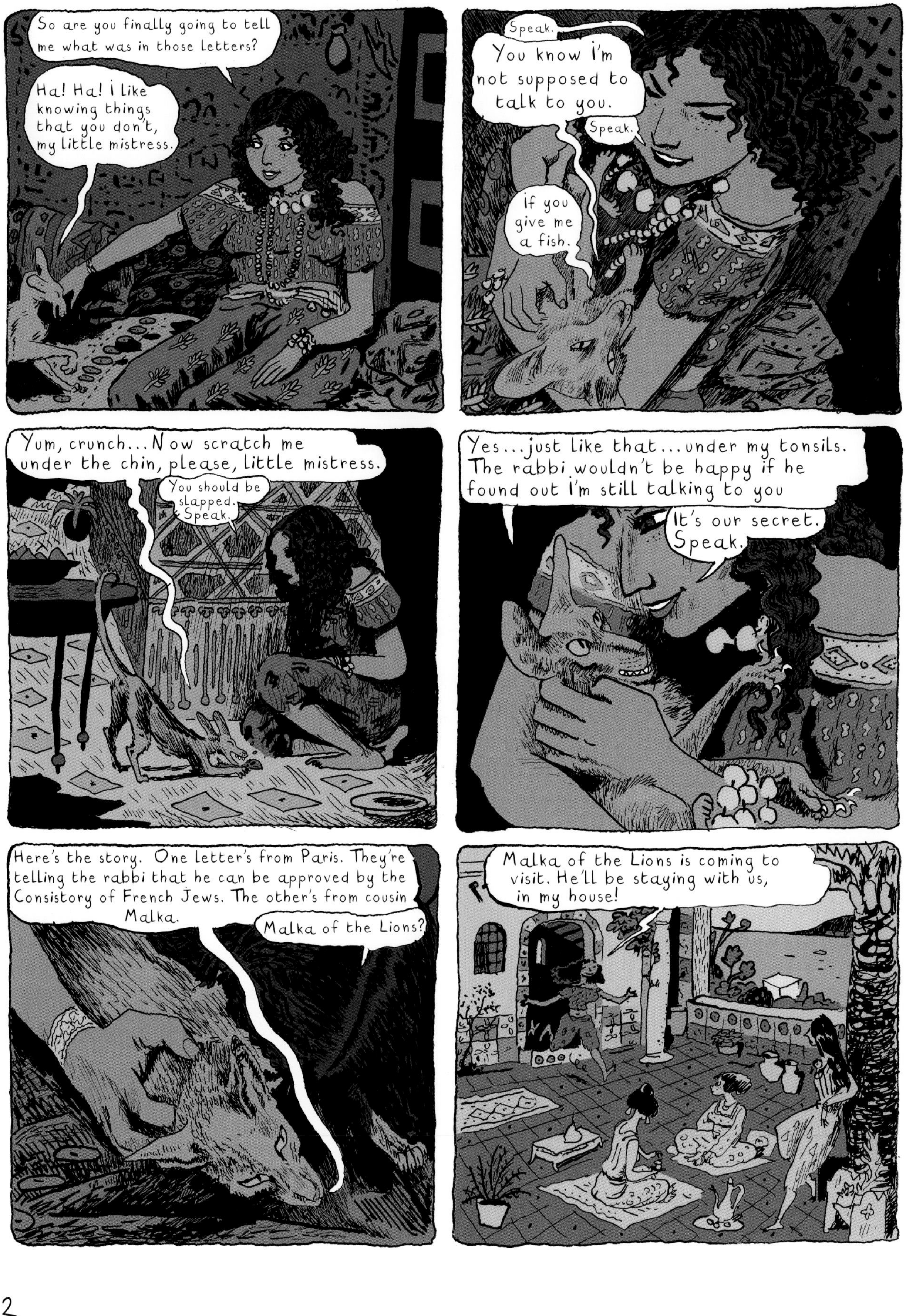
So are you finally going to tell me what was in those letters?
Ha! Ha! I like knowing things that you don't, my little mistress.
Speak.
You know I'm not supposed to talk to you.
Speak.
If you give me a fish.
Yum, crunch... Now scratch me under the chin, please, little mistress.
You should be slapped. Speak.
Yes... just like that... under my tonsils. The rabbi wouldn't be happy if he found out I'm still talking to you
It's our secret. Speak.
Here's the story. One letter's from Paris. They're telling the rabbi that he can be approved by the Consistory of French Jews. The other's from cousin Malka.
Malka of the Lions?
Malka of the Lions is coming to visit. He'll be staying with us, in my house!

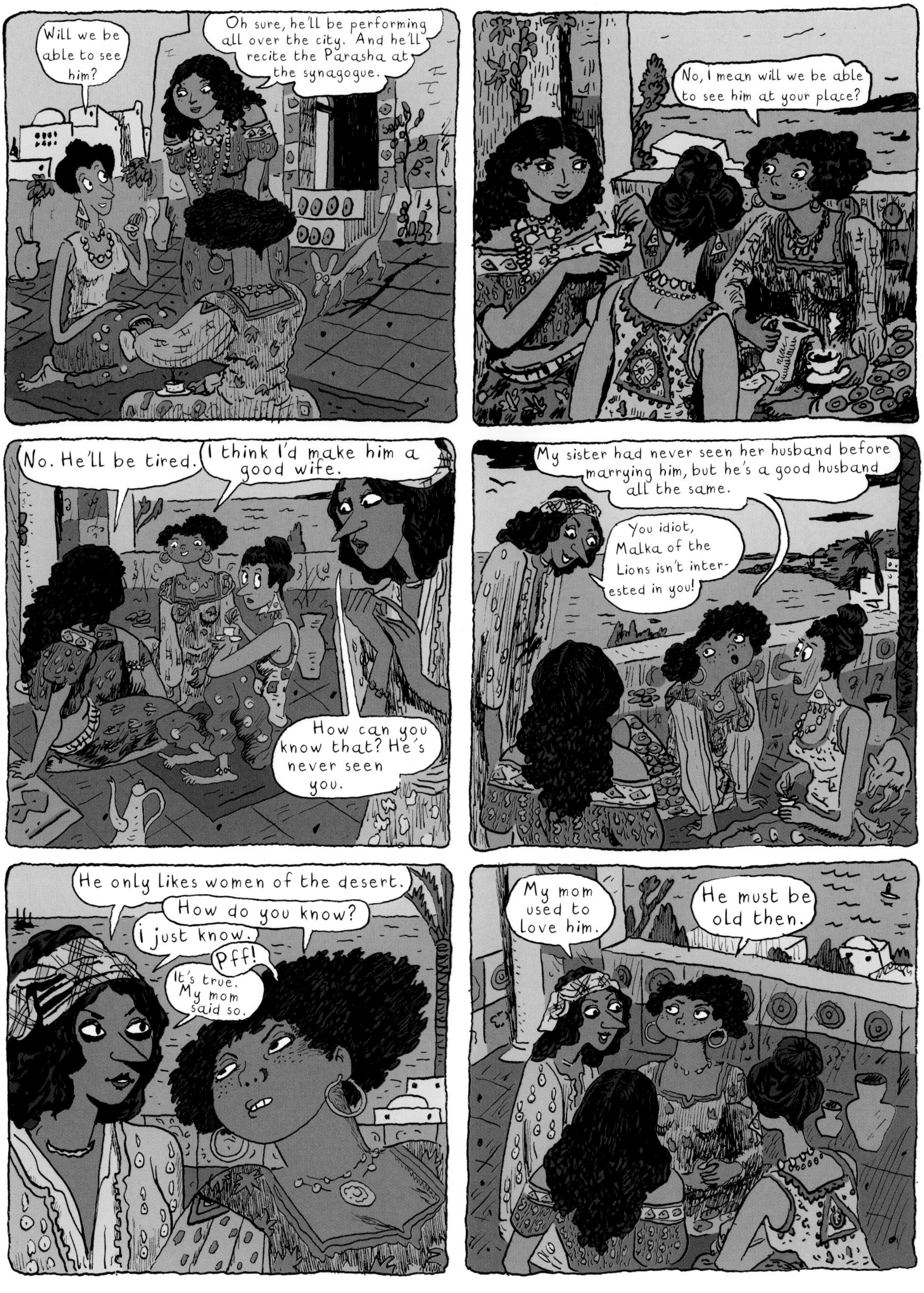
Will we be able to see him?
Oh sure, he'll be performing all over the city. And he'll recite the Parasha at the synagogue.
No, I mean will we be able to see him at your place?
No. He'll be tired.
I think I'd make him a good wife.
How can you know that? He's never seen you.
My sister had never seen her husband before marrying him, but he's a good husband all the same.
You idiot, Malka of the Lions isn't interested in you!
He only likes women of the desert.
How do you know?
I just know.
Pff!
It's true. My mom said so.
My mom used to love him.
He must be old then.

Shut up! I'm going to tell you a story about Malka of the Lions.

One night he was singing psalms in an oasis while playing the lute.

He wasn't riding a white horse, while you're at it?

Yeah.

HA! HA! HA! HA!

Oh, you're so dumb.

He was in this oasis and there was a camp.

Bedouins?

English people, from Gibraltar. Anyway, a woman's scream rings out from one of the tents.

The other English people weren't there?

No. Shut up.

I know this story of yours. There was a lion in the tent, and Malka walked in and saved the woman.

You don't know a thing.

The woman was naked, believe it or not.

Non-Jewish women are always naked.

Totally naked?

Yes, and covered in soap.

So to avoid offending her, Malka entered the tent with his eyes closed.

And with his eyes closed, he tamed the lion and led him out.

And how long after that did Malka leave the Englishwoman's tent?

I'm telling you his eyes were closed. He left the tent just as if there had been a man inside.

He didn't make any stupid comments or pull any playboy tricks.

I believe you. He's a pious man.

My guess is he wouldn't care about a woman who's covered in soap and afraid of lions.

55

You know, mistress, I know the real version of this story. At least, one version.

What do you mean?

Well, it happened several times. It turns out that this lion—he's an old lion—is a friend of Malka's. He spoke to me.

It's their little act. The lion scares someone, then Malka turns up unexpectedly and saves the day.

Sometimes all he gets is the glory. But other times he's given money or gifts.

And when it's ladies...

That's enough!

What, you don't want to hear the rest?

Another word and I'll tell Daddy that you're talking to me.

Meow!

Zlabya.

Yes, Daddy.

Zlabya, lend me some books in French.

What do you need those books for, Daddy?

For a dictation.

I'm going to become the official rabbi of our community.

But Dad, you're already the rabbi.

No. Right now, I'm rabbi just like that, but if I pass this dictation I'll be approved by the Consistory of French Jews.

And the Consistory will name me as the official rabbi.

Why is it any business of the French who gets to be rabbi here? And why do they want to make you do a dictation?

To see if I'm suitable. You don't want them to let just anyone be official rabbi, do you?

Well, I find it insulting that they're making you do a dictation.

Ah, what do you know? Give me some books.

57

And you, stop looking at me like an idiot.

Here, make yourself useful. Read to me!

OK..."Daphnis and Alcimadura..."

What's that?

That's the title.

A fable by La Fontaine has a title like that?

Yes.

Choose another one.

Okay.

"The Taper."

Is that all you found? Another fable, hurry up.

Hmpf... "Jupiter and the Passenger." "Oh, what riches on the Gods would cascade..."

Gods, you said?

Yes.

No, that won't do.

Find me a monotheistic fable. With animals, normal animals whose names we know.

Fine. "The Cat, the Weasel, and the Young Rabbit."

How's that?

Good.

Because if you want I can look for a fable with only kosher animals.

Ah! Shut up and read.

Should I shut up or read?

Read.

Hmm... "The house where Jack Rabbit was born was taken over early, one lovely morn."

Hang on, hang on.

"This do-es gre-at-ly re-sem-ble the so-me-ti-me dee-baaatesss..."

Why are you talking funny?

"...the sometime debates that little lords bring along to heads of states."

Uh-oh!

"to he-ads of sta-ate."

There. I'm done.

Well?

Listen, master ...

You'll never manage without me.

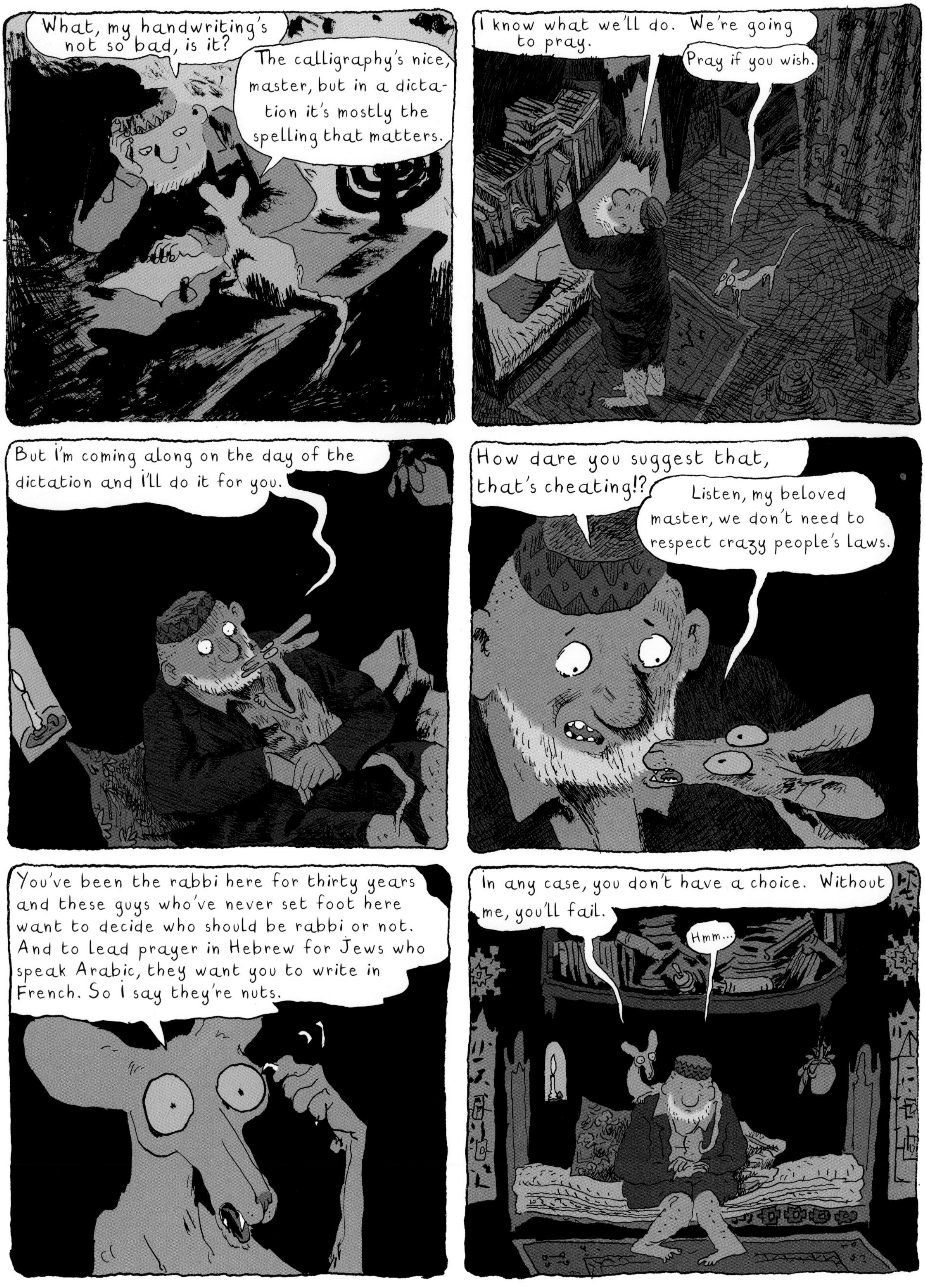
What, my handwriting's not so bad, is it?
The calligraphy's nice, master, but in a dictation it's mostly the spelling that matters.
I know what we'll do. We're going to pray.
Pray if you wish.
But I'm coming along on the day of the dictation and I'll do it for you.
How dare you suggest that, that's cheating!?
Listen, my beloved master, we don't need to respect crazy people's laws.
You've been the rabbi here for thirty years and these guys who've never set foot here want to decide who should be rabbi or not. And to lead prayer in Hebrew for Jews who speak Arabic, they want you to write in French. So I say they're nuts.
In any case, you don't have a choice. Without me, you'll fail.
Hmm...

The spelling test takes place in a school.

I thought there'd be other rabbis, but there's just us and the administrative people.

They won't let me in. They say animals aren't allowed in the school.

What a strange cat!

Come in, come in, but the cat stays outside.

My master says I am the reincarnation of his ancestor who was a miracle-working rabbi and whose great-grand-uncle carried the slippers of Rabbi Simeon bar Yohai.

No, no, not per-mitted.

Tick! Tock! Tick!

C'mon, let's get started.

That doesn't sway them. They say no cat.

My master enters the school without me.

61

From the window I see my master in the classroom. The clerk is giving the dictation.

My master asks the man whether he could please speak more slowly.

I see my master biting his thumb and crossing things out.

He's not going to make it.

"Thou shalt not invoke the Lord's name in vain."

It's not in vain. I'm going to perform an act of sacrilegious magic.

Among Jews, you only speak the Lord's name during actual prayers.

When you learn the prayers, you don't say "Adonai" but "Adoshem," to avoid speaking the true sacred name.

Even "Our Lord," "Eloheinu," you don't really say; we say "Elokeinu," as if outside of prayer we had as much water in our mouths as Pharaoh drowning in the Red Sea.

When we write the name of God, we have to be sure that the paper on which it is written will never be thrown out. Any paper on which the name of God is written is like a living being.

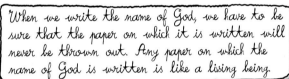

When prayer books are old and unusable we carry them to the graveyard for burial as if they were old sages. Anyone who burns a book or the Torah will be judged as harshly as the worst murderer.

Nothing can excuse or expunge his crime, neither passion nor ignorance.

63

One day when I was a young cat there was an Arab riot.

CRASH! BANG! CRASH!

Daddy, what's happening?

They were upset with the French, but since the French were too strong they showed up in the Jewish neighborhood with pikes and rifles.

It's nothing, darling. It's just people having a good time in the street. Don't worry.

Janissaries came to get us and take us to a safe place. They brought us to a warehouse and set up barricades.

Night was starting to fall. We heard screams outside and smelled smoke.

My master said he had to go out because some of his books weren't safe. The Janissary didn't let him.

Are you out of your mind?

So my master got angry and even Zlabya wasn't able to calm him down.

My master went to see the head Janissary and told him that among his books there were treasures. The chief asked whether my master had sacred books. My master said yes.

The Janissary, who was an educated man, asked whether he had the Kabbalah or magical formulas or spells. My master said yes, but that the most sacred book was his prayer book.

My master said this was the book that his father had used to say his prayers three times a day throughout his life.

The head Janissary took my master by the arm and both of them went out into the street to find the book.

And my master, who loves books so much, is failing his dictation.

We need a miracle.

65

I don't care if it's forbidden, I invoke the name of God.

Adonai, Adonai.

Adonai. Adonai. Adonai.

Adonai. Adonai. Meow.

What?

Meow.

What is happening to me?

Meow.

My master comes out. I don't like the look on his face.

I ask him if it went okay.

What?

Meow?

He doesn't feel much like talking, I think.

Meow!
Meow!
Meow!

Oh, if you think I'm in the mood for your silliness.

So how did it go?

Meow.

You can talk, no one can hear you.

Meow.

Meow! Meow! Meow! Me-meow! Meow!

Daddy! I think the cat can't speak anymore.

What, you're talking to the cat?

No, but he's meowing.

Let him meow.

It didn't go well, did it?

I don't know.

I did my best, but I don't think it'll be good enough.

67

My master isn't doing well. Since the dictation, he has no enthusiasm for anything.

He doesn't even care about things that used to make us laugh.

Like the goats climbing up the acacia trees to graze. Before, he would say, "Look, a goat tree." "When they're ripe, the fruits will fall."

But these days he walks past it without seeing it. The truth is, he's afraid of receiving a letter telling him that he's no longer the rabbi.

And every morning he's afraid when he hears the postman's bicycle. Actually, he doesn't even need a letter. He already knows it's hopeless.

And now that I can no longer speak, there's nothing I can do about it.

This morning the postman brings a letter for my master. A letter from France like the one for the dictation. The rabbi hides it in his pocket. He doesn't want to open it.

Nothing will spoil this day for me, he says. Today cousin Malka is in town.

Is he coming to the house, Daddy?

No, I'm meeting him in town.

Where?

At the Carbodel café.

But he's crazy! We're going to get our asses kicked!

Mazel tov ve siman tov...

...Yehe lanu...

Yehe lanu Ye lanu...

My master passes in front of the café but doesn't stop.

Then he hides a little on the street corner. He watches.

69

I get it! He's waiting for the cousin to come, because the cousin has a rifle and a lion.

And when cousin Malka sits down, the guy doesn't dare tell him "Jews aren't welcome." All he says is "What will it be?" Because of the lion and rifle, of course.

And also because Malka of the Lions has a particular way of looking at you that makes you not want to say no to him.

My master jumps into his cousin's arms and issues blessings in Arabic, Ladino, and the Algerian Pataouete slang. The hugging lasts a good five minutes.

Ha! Ha! Ha!

Ha! Ha!

Then because he's a bit of a coward, my master gives a little obsequious greeting to the waiter, who doesn't dare say anything but looks pretty convinced that my master is making fun of him.

You're so handsome, God bless!

It's not too obvious?

What?

That I dyed my mustache.

Ha! Ha! Say "five."

Are you kidding? You look twenty.

Hamsa! Hamsa!

Ah, come on.

My cousin, may God keep you until you're a hundred and twenty.

I swear on my life, Cousin, time has no effect on you.

With you also, and may he keep your daughter.

Or on you—you're thinner, aren't you?

And your lion, too, all of us happy together.

No. You're handsome anyway.

And in health.

Amen.

Amen.

I say hello to the old lion. At least he understands me. I can still speak to animals. That's something.

Shalom, old friend.

Shalom, big guy.

The rabbi tells Malka about the dictation disaster.

Don't worry, you'll always be the rabbi.

No, it'll be like in Oran. A pale-faced rabbi with no beard and lace-up shoes will come from France and take my place.

He'll have horrible features like freckles and Polish teeth. He'll smell like a corpse and conduct prayers in my place.

Instead of a he'll say o and he won't know our songs and they'll keep me only to cut chickens' throats and for circumcisions because French rabbis are afraid of blood.

If that's so, I'll cut his throat myself.

You're so nice. Ask for some more anisette, Cousin.

With lupins and mixed olives, but you ask, my cousin, because I'm afraid of this nasty waiter.

RRR RRR

Rabbi! Rabbi!

Ah, but this one, no Pole will ever rid me of him....

Rabbi, it's old Sasson Corcos, he's dying. We need prayers.

Come along.

With the Lion?

Yes. Your Lion brings luck.

What about me? Ever since I stopped speaking, it's as if I wasn't there.

Has the doctor come?

Yes, he's at his bedside. He says the old man should have died a long time ago.

For three days, he was in pain and he kept repeating "Leave me alone" and "When God loves you, he doesn't do this to you." And then he calmed down.

Now it's as if he were dead, but he's alive.

I don't understand a thing. This man is dead but his eyes stay open. He no longer breathes but he moves, he forms words, he swallows.

He's waiting for someone.

Is there a member of the family who isn't here but is expected?

Yes.

There's his grandson. He is coming specially from France. He should be here any moment.

And they're very close?

Yes, he loves him.

So we'll just wait for him.

73

The grandson arrived. Boy, did he look shaken! It looked like he hadn't stopped crying throughout the entire trip.

He took the old man's hand and the old man looked up at him and the old man's head dropped to his chest.

The grandson closed his eyes and everyone said the Shema.

Shema Yisrael...

Shema Yisrael...

...Adonai Eloheinu Adonai Echad...

Shema Yisrael Adonai Eloheinu Adonai Echad

Baruch Shem Kevod Malchuto Le'olam Va'ed

Baruch Shem Kevod Malchuto Le'olam Va'ed

"All goes to the same place. All is dust and all goes to dust," says the rabbi. "We form a circle around the deceased so nothing harmful can enter him from outside.

The dead are vulnerable until their burial. We have to protect them. We light a candle.

The women of the family come in and they all start to wail. Some of them tear at their faces with their nails. The lion and I are quite disturbed by this display.

The rabbi wants to start reading psalms, but the grandson says they have to do it another way.

Now open your books to page...

No.

That's not the way it's done where we come from.

They're a Moroccan family, their rites are different from ours. We do it the way they're used to, following the grandson's instructions.

Cover the mirror completely, Auntie.

We do the same thing.

Leave it, Cousin.

We undress the body and place him on the ground, under a shroud. That's how we do it. We cover all the mirrors in the house, which is also the way we do it.

Did you see, the people aren't afraid of you. You'd think it's normal for them to see a lion.

I don't see what's so unusual about my presence.

know, I find it a shocking to see animals in the house.

I don't somehow see Little inside

The grandson makes us empty all containers in which there is water. He sends a boy to let the neighbors know that a person has died and that they should throw out their water, too.

The rabbi asks why we're doing this. It's because the Angel of Death is on the prowl and could dip his sword in this water, the young man answers.

What he's saying, that's not real religion, just superstition, right? But if it makes him happy we should let it go.

That's right.

Meanwhile, the people of the community start preparing the tomb, because the burial must take place as quickly as possible. In the meantime, we stay in a circle around the deceased and pray all night long.

75

In the morning, the grandfather crosses town to the sound of the shofar. "What must people be thinking, seeing these Jews going to the cemetery led by a lion and a cat?

We get to the cemetery and I was expecting that we'd get down to burying this grandfather, but no. They start circling around the coffin.

The lion asks me what this is all about; I tell him that if I could speak I'd ask the rabbi, but I can't talk to humans anymore.

Finally, we bury him. Someone brought some earth from Israel and each person throws a little on the dead man. They say prayers and it's over.

The grandson says we have to go pretty quickly so we don't hear the dead man's voice calling us.

Of course, I make a point of retracing my steps to listen, but I don't hear anything.

Everyone goes back to the dead man's home to have something to eat. I'm hungry, too, but I don't dare meow under the circumstances.

They don't give me or the lion anything. But I think the lion's used to not eating.

Here, try the raisin rolls.

After that, the rabbi and Malka leave the house of the grieving family. The grandson follows them.

Excuse me

He has a small suitcase. He asks for the address of the Sadi Carnot Hotel.

I don't know the city very well. Could you show me how to get to the Sadi Carnot Hotel?

He explains that his grandfather's house is small and that part of the family came from far away; that's why he's going to a hotel.

You can't be serious, my son. You're not going to a hotel on a day like today.

I promise you, it doesn't bother me.

It's out of the question.

The rabbi says the young man will come sleep at our house.

You're coming home with us, it will be my pleasure. You'll be comfortable there.

Are you sure?

Of course.

I don't know about this guy.

What're you talking about?

I dunno, he's too uptight.

Tch, nonsense!

Cats feel these things.

77

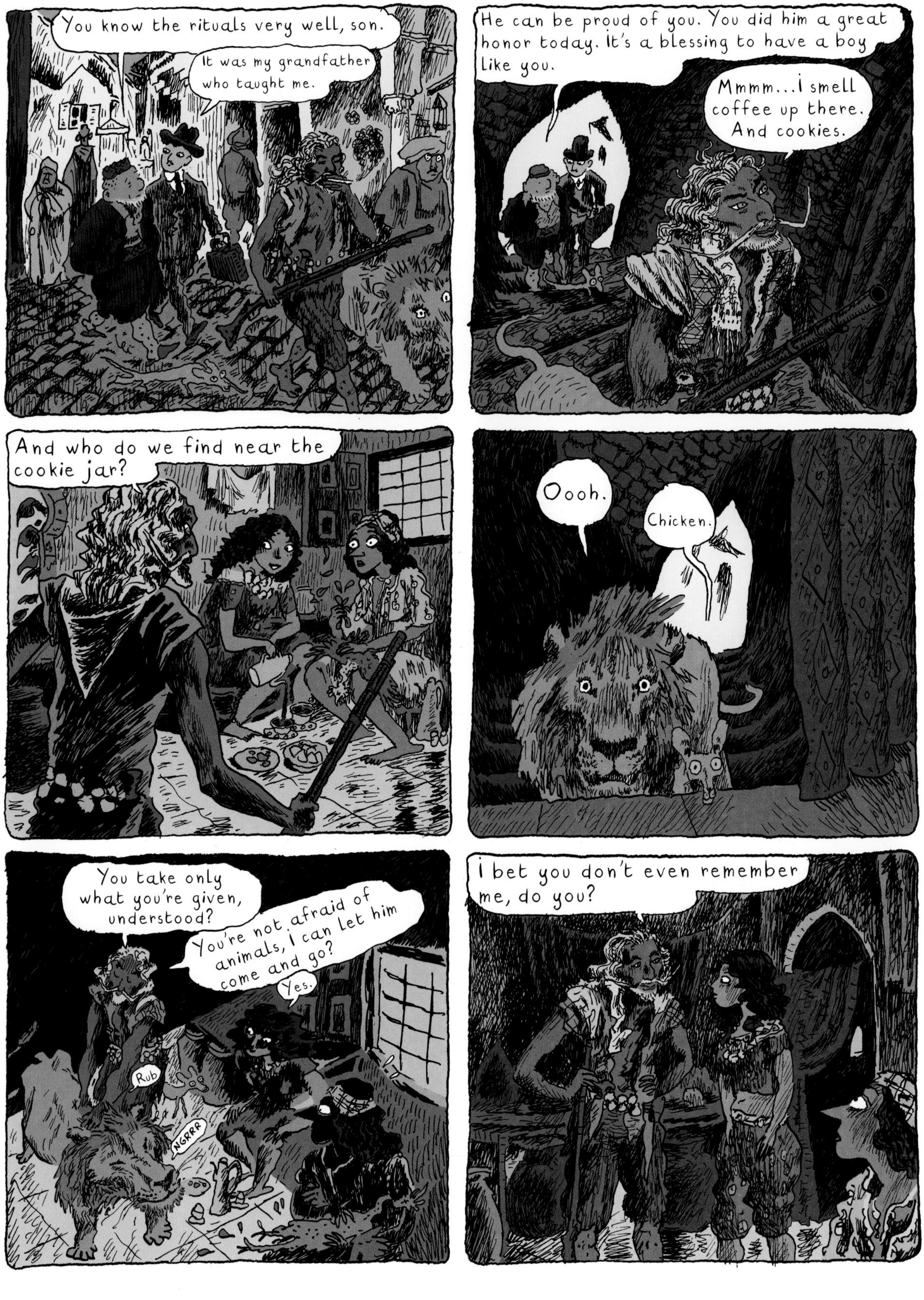
You know the rituals very well, son.
It was my grandfather who taught me.
He can be proud of you. You did him a great honor today. It's a blessing to have a boy like you.
Mmmm...I smell coffee up there. And cookies.
And who do we find near the cookie jar?
Oooh.
Chicken.
You take only what you're given, understood?
You're not afraid of animals, I can let him come and go?
Yes.
Rub
NGRRR
I bet you don't even remember me, do you?

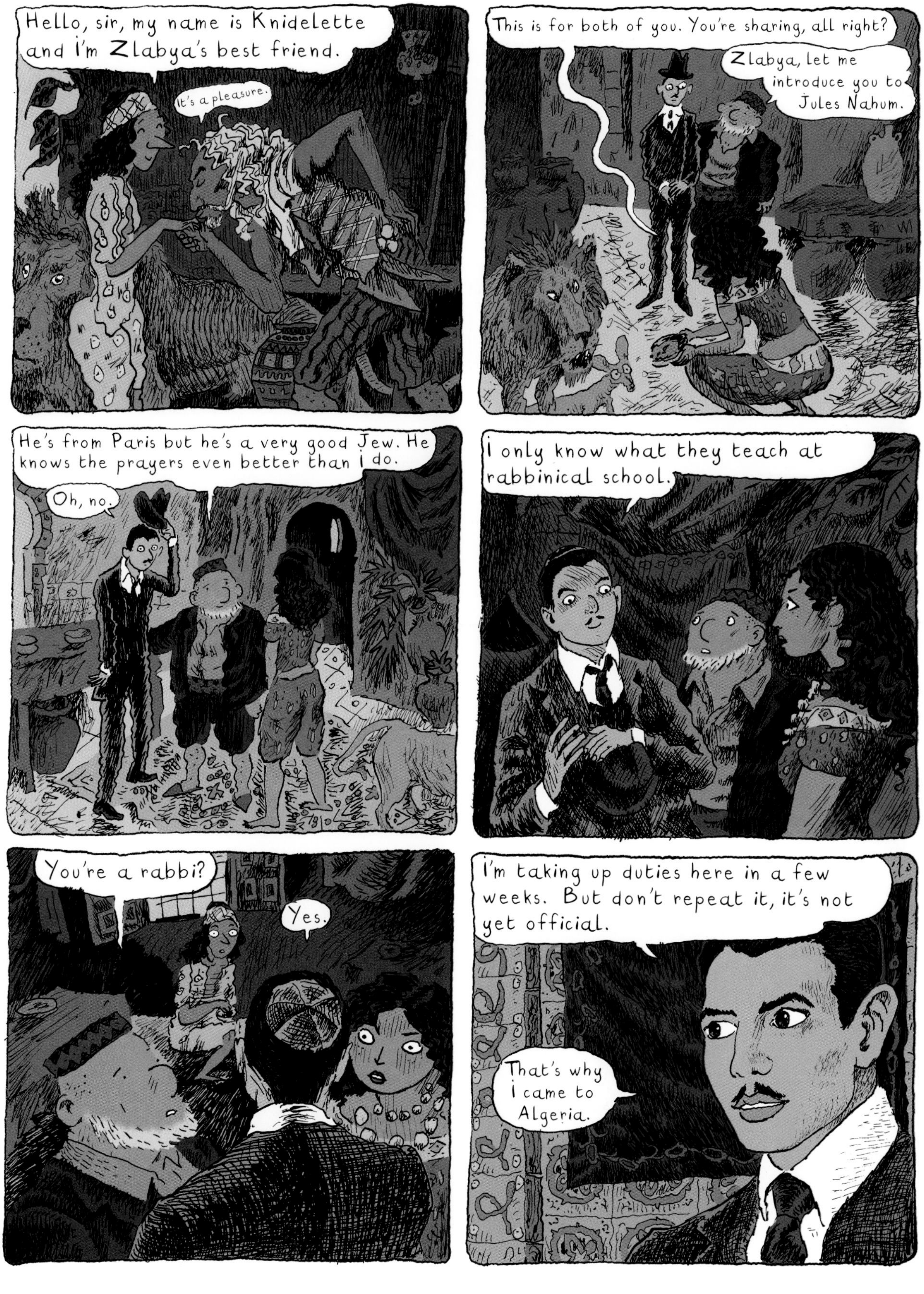
Hello, sir, my name is Knidelette and I'm Zlabya's best friend.
It's a pleasure.
This is for both of you. You're sharing, all right?
Zlabya, let me introduce you to Jules Nahum.
He's from Paris but he's a very good Jew. He knows the prayers even better than I do.
Oh, no.
I only know what they teach at rabbinical school.
You're a rabbi?
Yes.
I'm taking up duties here in a few weeks. But don't repeat it, it's not yet official.
That's why I came to Algeria.

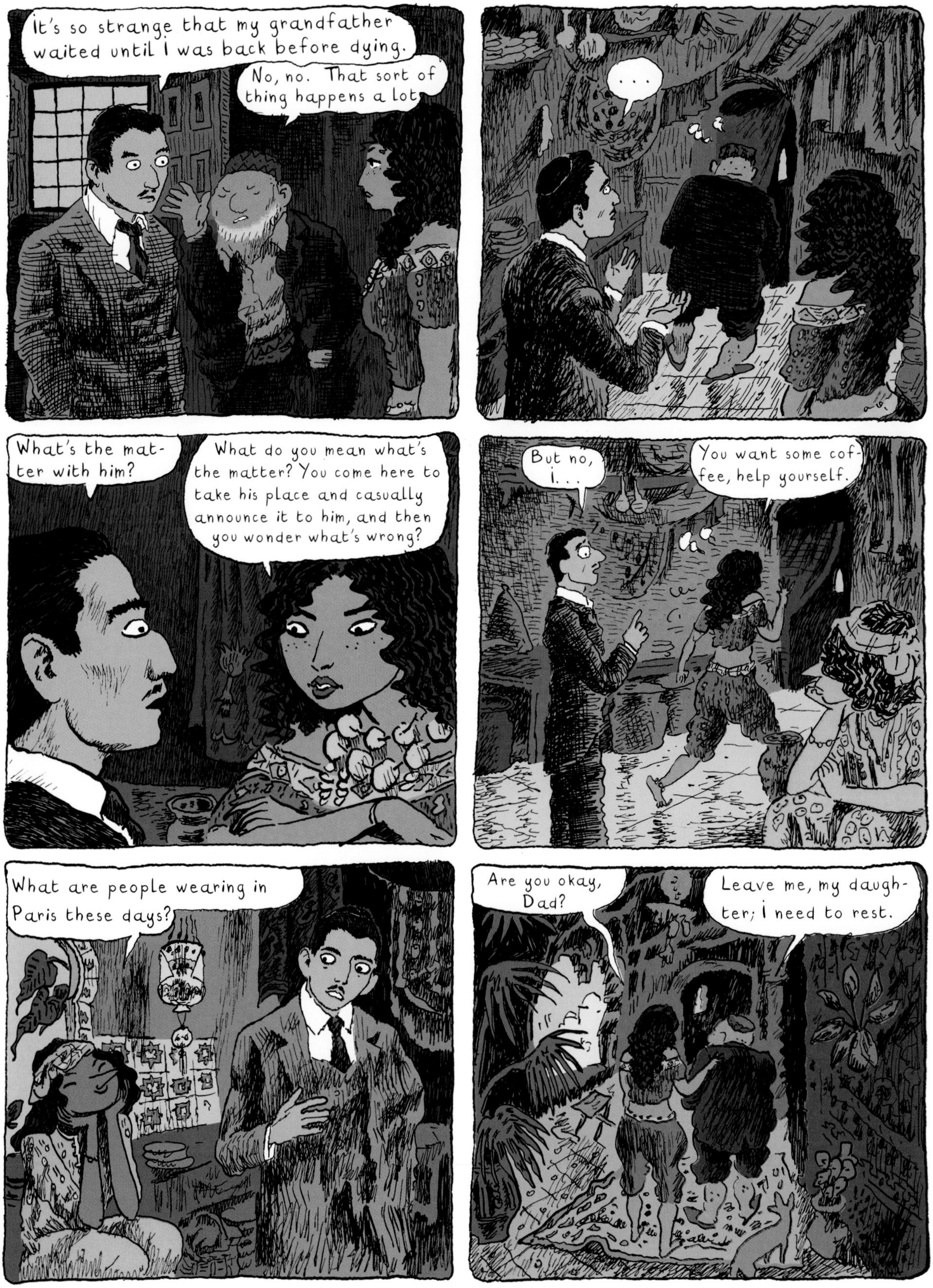
It's so strange that my grandfather waited until I was back before dying.
No, no. That sort of thing happens a lot.
. . .
What's the matter with him?
What do you mean what's the matter? You come here to take his place and casually announce it to him, and then you wonder what's wrong?
But no, I . . .
You want some coffee, help yourself.
What are people wearing in Paris these days?
Are you okay, Dad?
Leave me, my daughter; I need to rest.

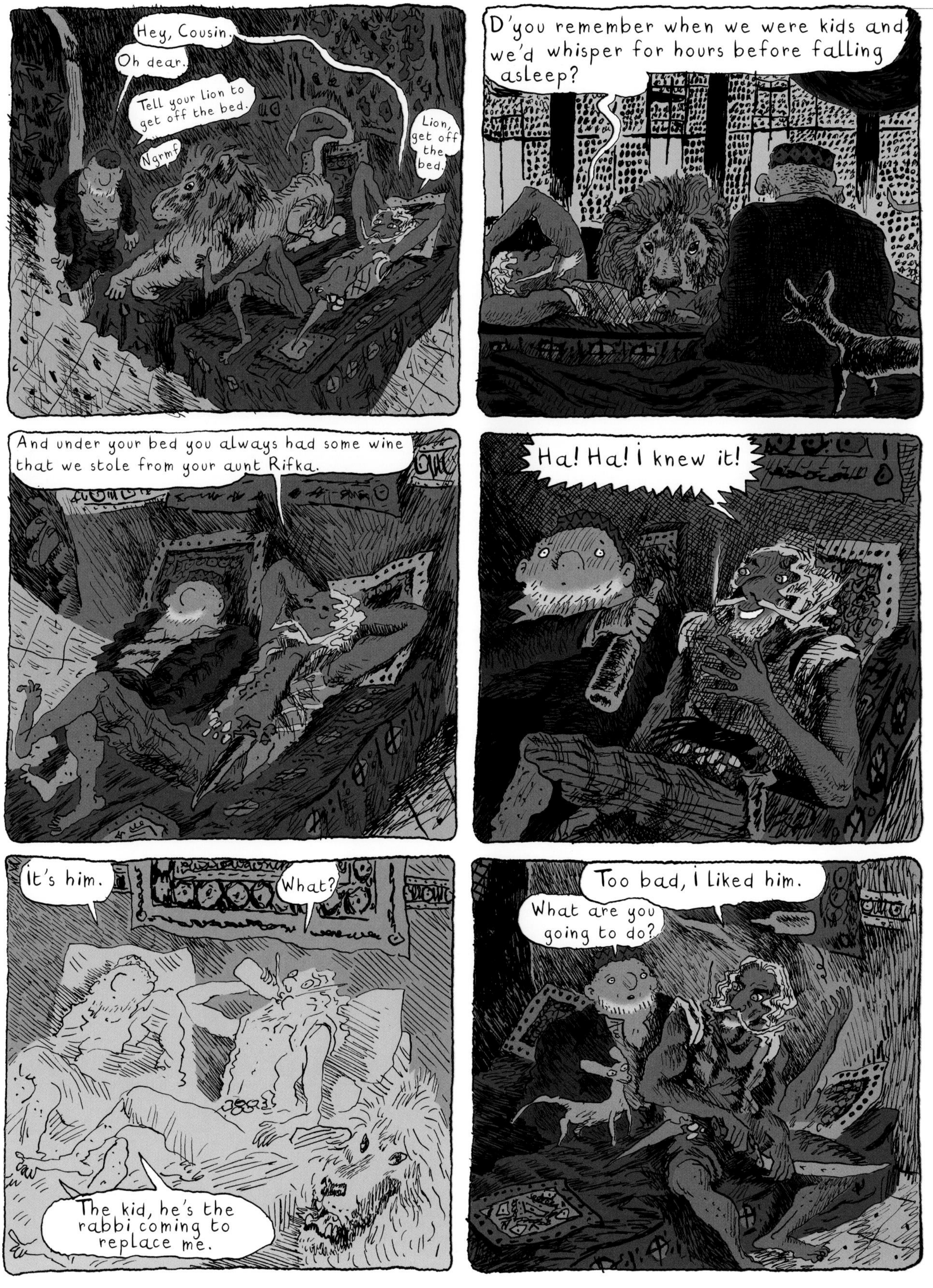
Hey, Cousin.
Oh dear.
Tell your lion to get off the bed.
Ngrmf
Lion, get off the bed.
D'you remember when we were kids and we'd whisper for hours before falling asleep?
And under your bed you always had some wine that we stole from your aunt Rifka.
Ha! Ha! I knew it!
It's him.
What?
The kid, he's the rabbi coming to replace me.
Too bad, I liked him.
What are you going to do?

Don't worry, I'll wait until there aren't any witnesses. And no one will find the body. I have a partner who takes care of what's left of my enemies.

No. You're really the sweetest cousin, but no. I'm going to leave for a few days, I have to think things through.

You're not going to do anything stupid, are you?

No, I'm going to the grave of Messaoud Sfar. It's his birthday and he always gives me good advice.

I'll be back in a few days.

You sure you don't want me to kill him? You know, sometimes you kill just one person and it takes care of everything.

You're kindness personified, my cousin, but no. Just watch over the house while I'm gone.

And keep my daughter far from that kid.

82

Messaoud Sfar was the father-in-law of the rabbi's grandfather. He was a doctor and a saint. We visit his grave every year.

On the road we pass an old Arab on a donkey. He greets us. My master offers perfumed water, the Arab offers milk. They seem to know each other.

Shalom aleichem.

Salaam aleikum.

The old man speaks the same kind of Arabic as the Jews do, literary Arabic. He must come from far away, because the Arabs here speak differently.

Kif al saha? Hamdullah

Shlonak? Hamdullah

Shlonak inti.

Salaam aleikum

Aleikum salaam

They decide to travel together. This allows me to talk to the donkey.

What's your master's name?

Where have you been? That's Sheikh Muhammad Sfar, the great singer.

He dances and his dancing makes people wise. He sings and his songs open eyes. He even makes donkeys smart.

Wait, an Arab is called SFAR?

Yes. Sfar's an Arab name.

83

Are you kidding? Sfar comes from "Sofer," which means "to write" in Hebrew. Sfar is a Jewish name.

You ass, Sfar comes from "yellow" in Arabic. It evokes the sulfur flower used by coppersmiths. Sfar's Arab through and through.

Besides, we're going to the grave of Messaoud Sfar, our ancestor.

That's where we're going, too.

Messaoud Sfar was a great Sufi, a saint.

No way! Messaoud Sfar was a rabbi.

Take that back!

Meow! Meow! Meow!

Hee-haw! Hee-haw! Hee-haw!

Looks like the animals are tired.

Yes. We'd better have a rest.

He's a strange ass. Believe it or not, he can read my scores and sings in three languages.

That's amazing!

It's more of a worry. He sings out of tune.

You can give speech to an ass, but he's still an ass.

You don't think we should educate everyone?

Yes, we should even educate asses. But without illusions.

Every time I like a song, I feel moved to pass it on. So I gather round the greatest possible number of musicians and teach it to them.

And that doesn't give them talent, does it?

No.

The worst part is that when I hear the text in their mouths, it's ruined. And the lyrics I liked become ordinary.

You know what, we should just live in a cave and mind our own business. I bring my books, you bring your songs.

No.

One day Allah would reproach us for it. We'd be like Jonah, who treated a tree as more important than people.

So what?

Aren't we allowed to say that we've done a lot for other people and that they've worn us out and we're old and we want to be left alone?

No.

85

Ah, but I tell you, my brother, I don't want to go home.

Why do you say that?

Thirty years I've been the rabbi. And now, without even coming to see me to soften the blow, they send me this letter from Paris to tell me I'm no longer the rabbi of anything at all.

Show me that letter.

Here, open it yourself.

You know the contents of letters before you've opened them?

This one I do.

Hmmm...you thought God was no longer with you and that's a great fault.

"Dear Rabbi, we are pleased to announce to you that you scored 55 out of 100 on your dictation." You did a dictation?

Read, read, brother.

Hmm ...

"You scored 55, which gives you the level of a primary-school diploma. The French Consistory is very proud of you and hopes that all the rabbis will follow your example and not remain asses who can't write French...."

They really wrote that?

No, I added the bit about asses.

So I'm still the rabbi! Oh, give me a hug! Come, let's pray.

Hey, watch out for my glasses!

Then they prayed, both of them. One facing Jerusalem, and the other Mecca.

And they danced.

The sheikh took his oud and lent the rabbi a tarbuka drum and they danced and sang and laughed and they couldn't have been more drunk if they'd been drinking.

And I told myself that, in this climate of euphoria, it wouldn't be a bad thing if I recovered my ability to speak.

But I didn't recover anything.

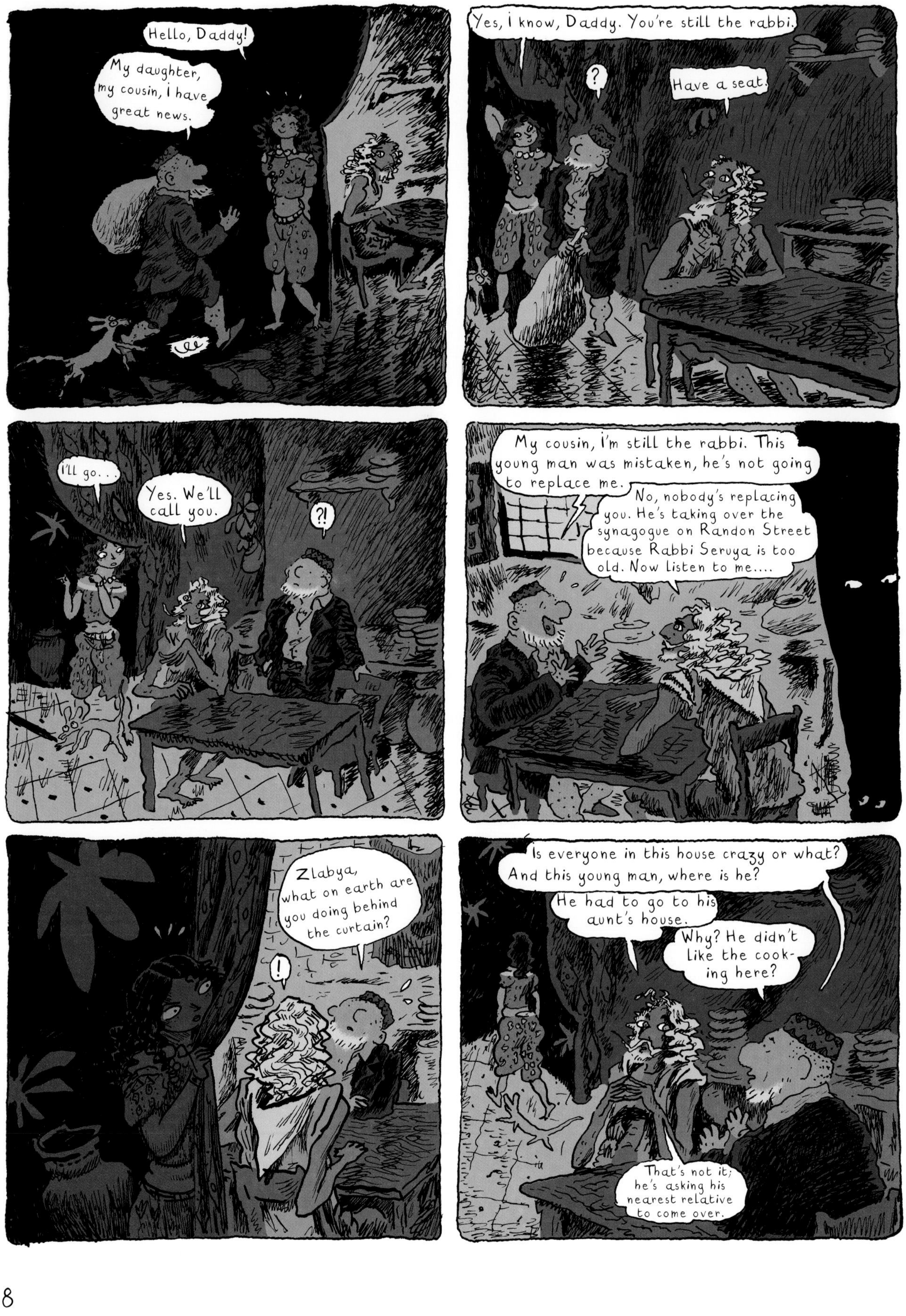
Hello, Daddy!
My daughter, my cousin, I have great news.
Yes, I know, Daddy. You're still the rabbi.
?
Have a seat.
I'll go...
Yes. We'll call you.
?!
My cousin, I'm still the rabbi. This young man was mistaken, he's not going to replace me.
No, nobody's replacing you. He's taking over the synagogue on Randon Street because Rabbi Seruya is too old. Now listen to me....
Zlabya, what on earth are you doing behind the curtain?
!
Is everyone in this house crazy or what? And this young man, where is he?
He had to go to his aunt's house.
Why? He didn't like the cooking here?
That's not it; he's asking his nearest relative to come over.

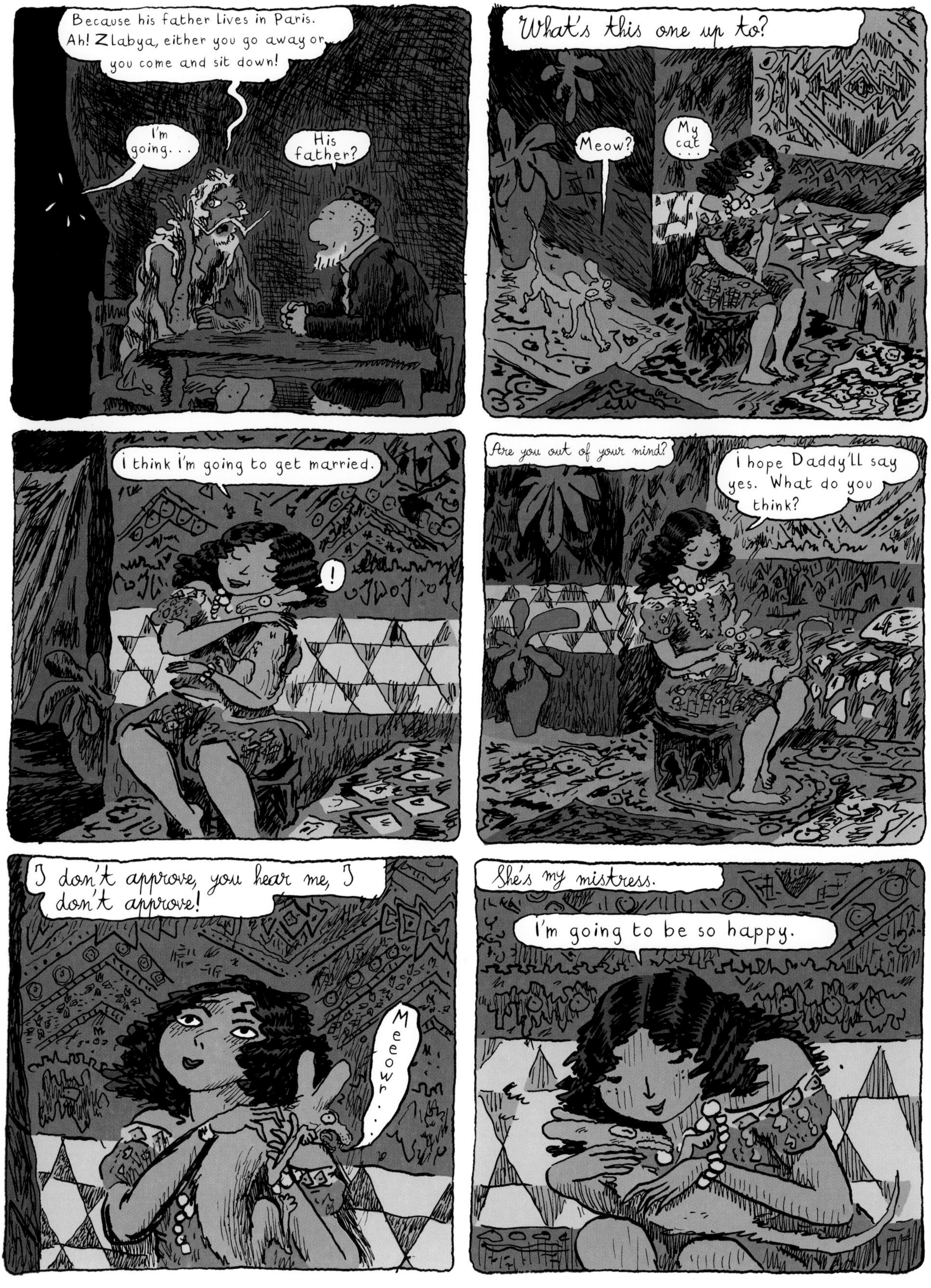
Because his father lives in Paris. Ah! Zlabya, either you go away or you come and sit down!
I'm going...
His father?
What's this one up to?
Meow?
My cat...
I think I'm going to get married.
!
Are you out of your mind?
I hope Daddy'll say yes. What do you think?
I don't approve, you hear me, I don't approve!
Meeowr...
She's my mistress.
I'm going to be so happy.

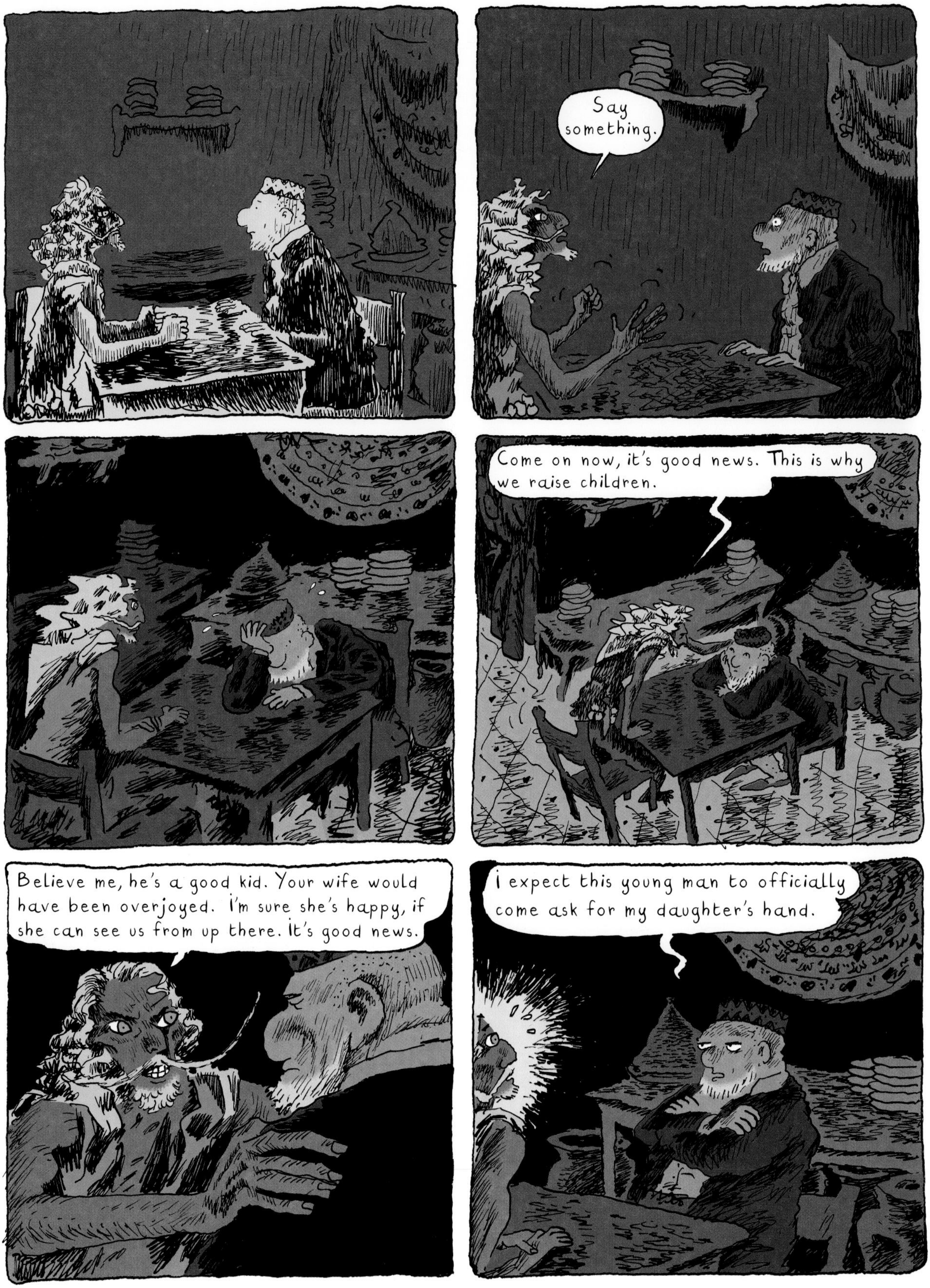
Say something.
Come on now, it's good news. This is why we raise children.
Believe me, he's a good kid. Your wife would have been overjoyed. I'm sure she's happy, if she can see us from up there. It's good news.
I expect this young man to officially come ask for my daughter's hand.

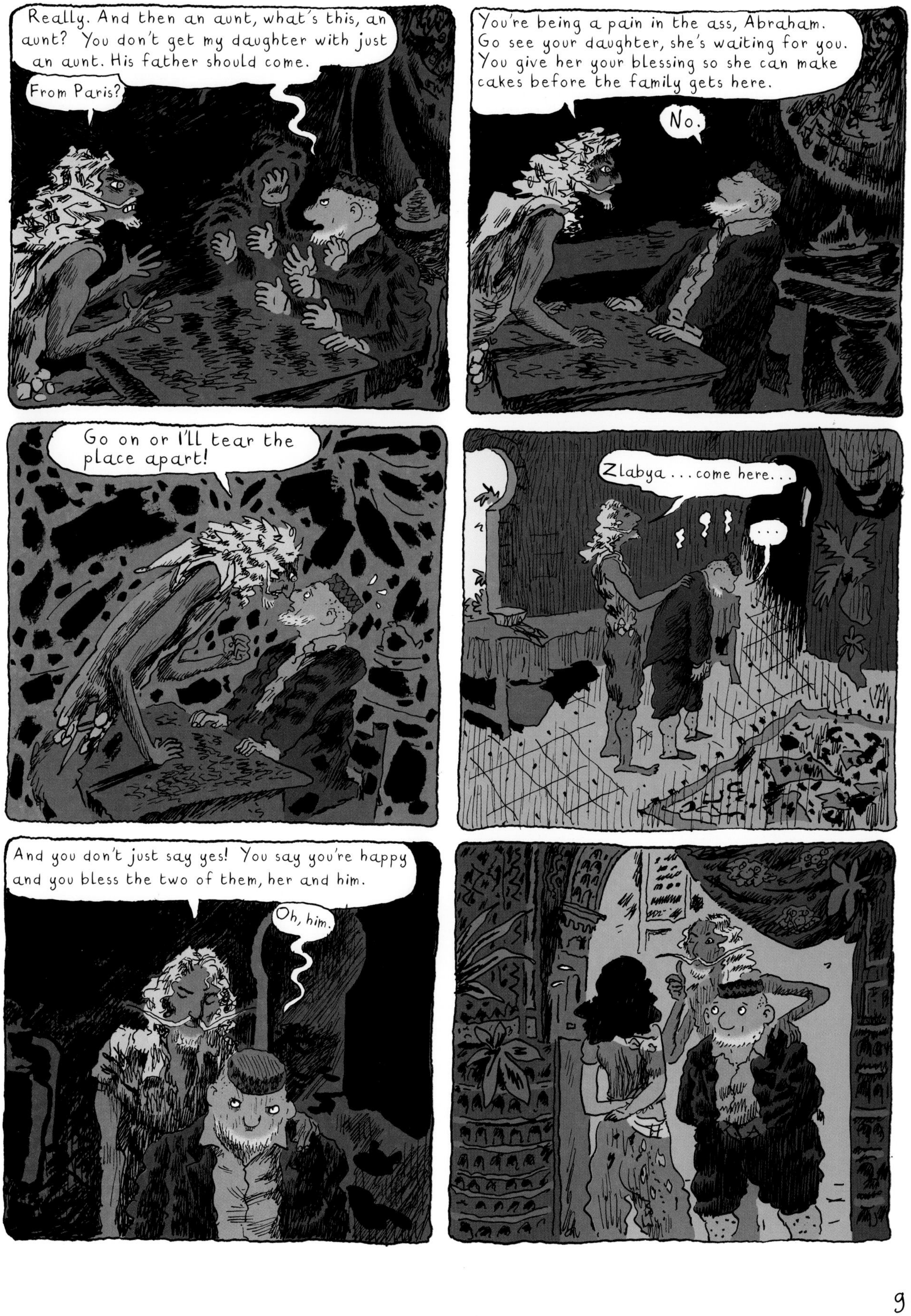
Really. And then an aunt, what's this, an aunt? You don't get my daughter with just an aunt. His father should come.
From Paris?
You're being a pain in the ass, Abraham. Go see your daughter, she's waiting for you. You give her your blessing so she can make cakes before the family gets here.
No.
Go on or I'll tear the place apart!
Zlabya . . . come here . . .
? ?
. . .
And you don't just say yes! You say you're happy and you bless the two of them, her and him.
Oh, him.

She's going to live at his place.

I haven't even been told if I'm going or not.

They ate cakes, cakes baked by my mistress. As if they were theirs.

And the young guy who kept looking at her with eyes that just begged to be clawed.

And my master who didn't say a thing.

He's taking your daughter from you.

He's going to take your daughter and you'll be old and she'll be pregnant and she'll be old and she'll have children who'll be old and everyone will die.

And you're letting this happen. What sort of master are you?

Sure, go ahead and feel sorry for yourself, now that everyone's left!

It was when they were here that you needed to react!

You should've said no, we want nothing to do with your mistress-and-daughter-stealing thief, harbinger of old age and swollen bellies and varicose veins. We want everything to stay just like it is.

But you just let things slide.

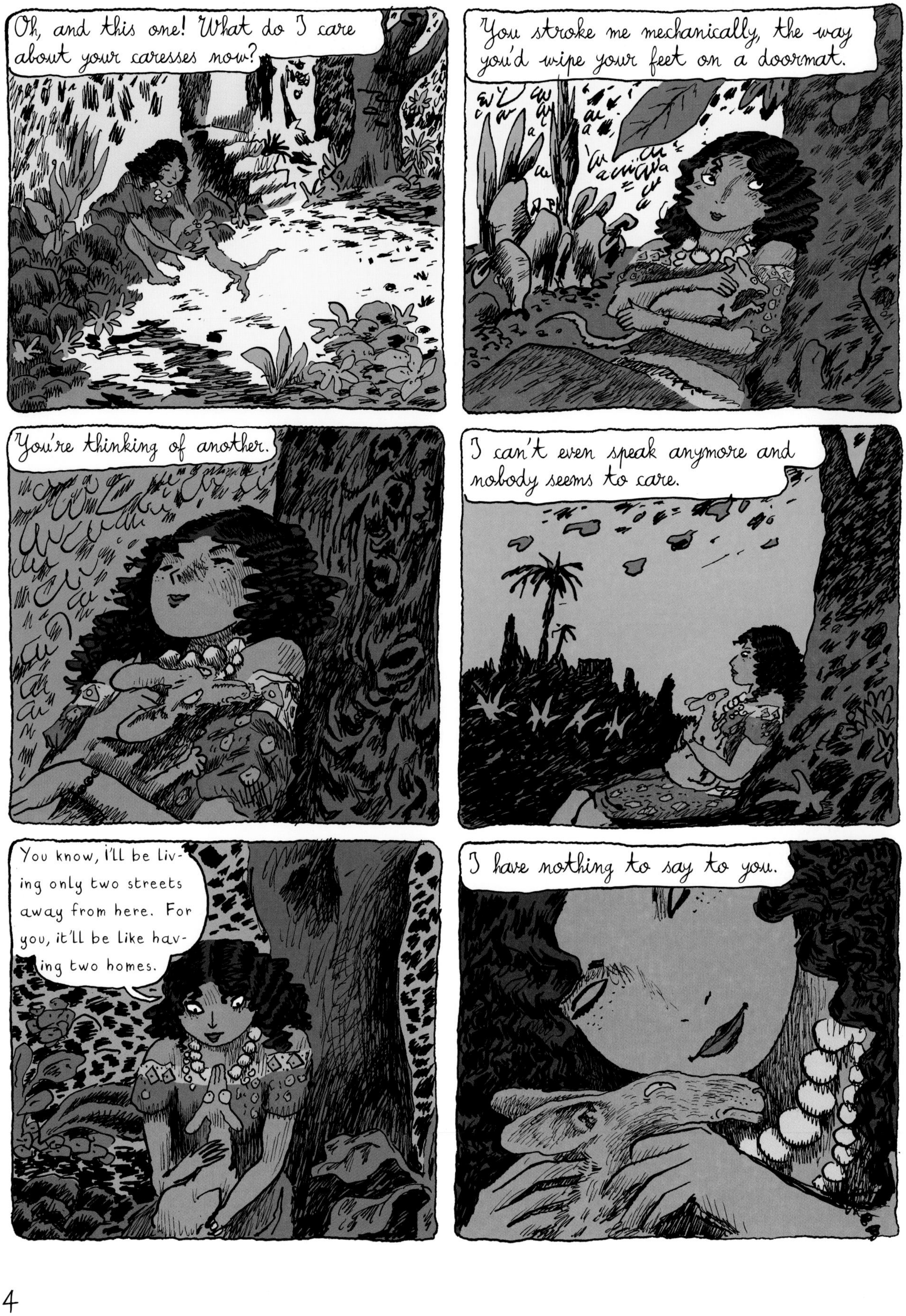
Oh, and this one! What do I care about your caresses now?
You stroke me mechanically, the way you'd wipe your feet on a doormat.
You're thinking of another.
I can't even speak anymore and nobody seems to care.
You know, I'll be living only two streets away from here. For you, it'll be like having two homes.
I have nothing to say to you.

3.

EXODUS

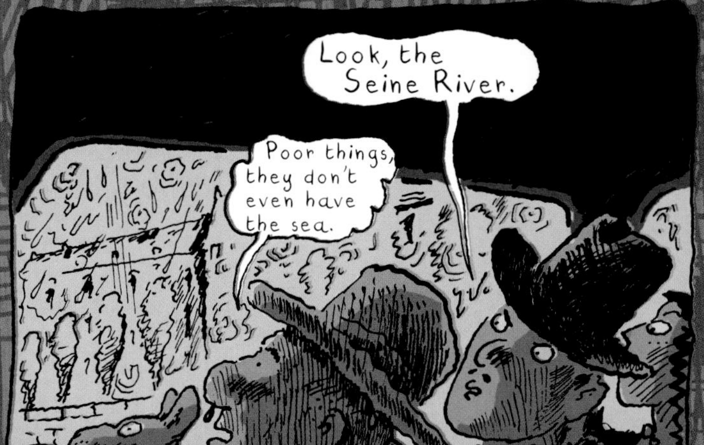
Poor things, they don't even have the sea.
Look, the Seine River.

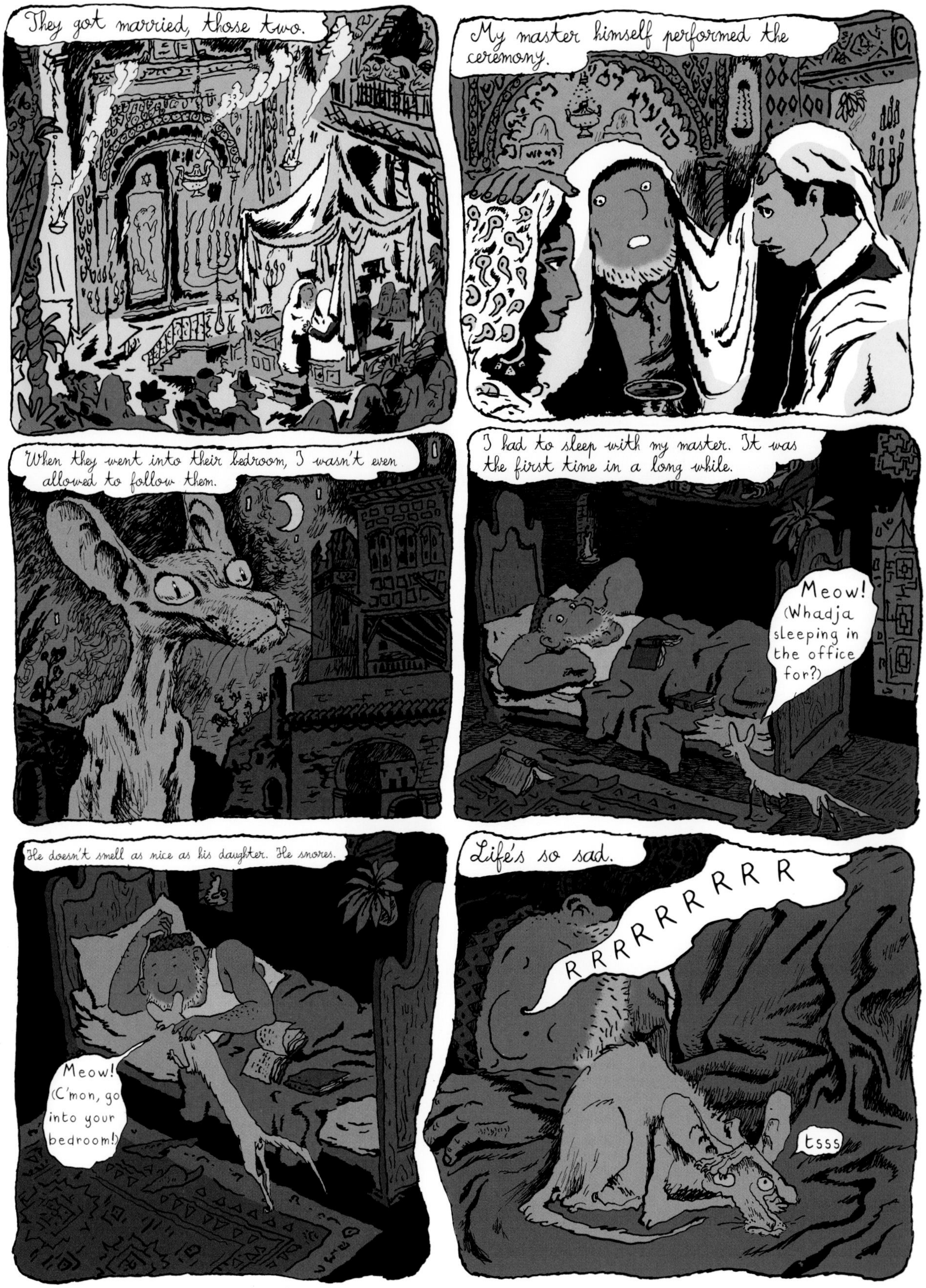
They got married, those two.
My master himself performed the ceremony.
When they went into their bedroom, I wasn't even allowed to follow them.
I had to sleep with my master. It was the first time in a long while.
Meow! (Whadja sleeping in the office for?)
He doesn't smell as nice as his daughter. He snores.
Meow! (C'mon, go into your bedroom!)
Life's so sad.
RRRRRRRRRRR
tsss

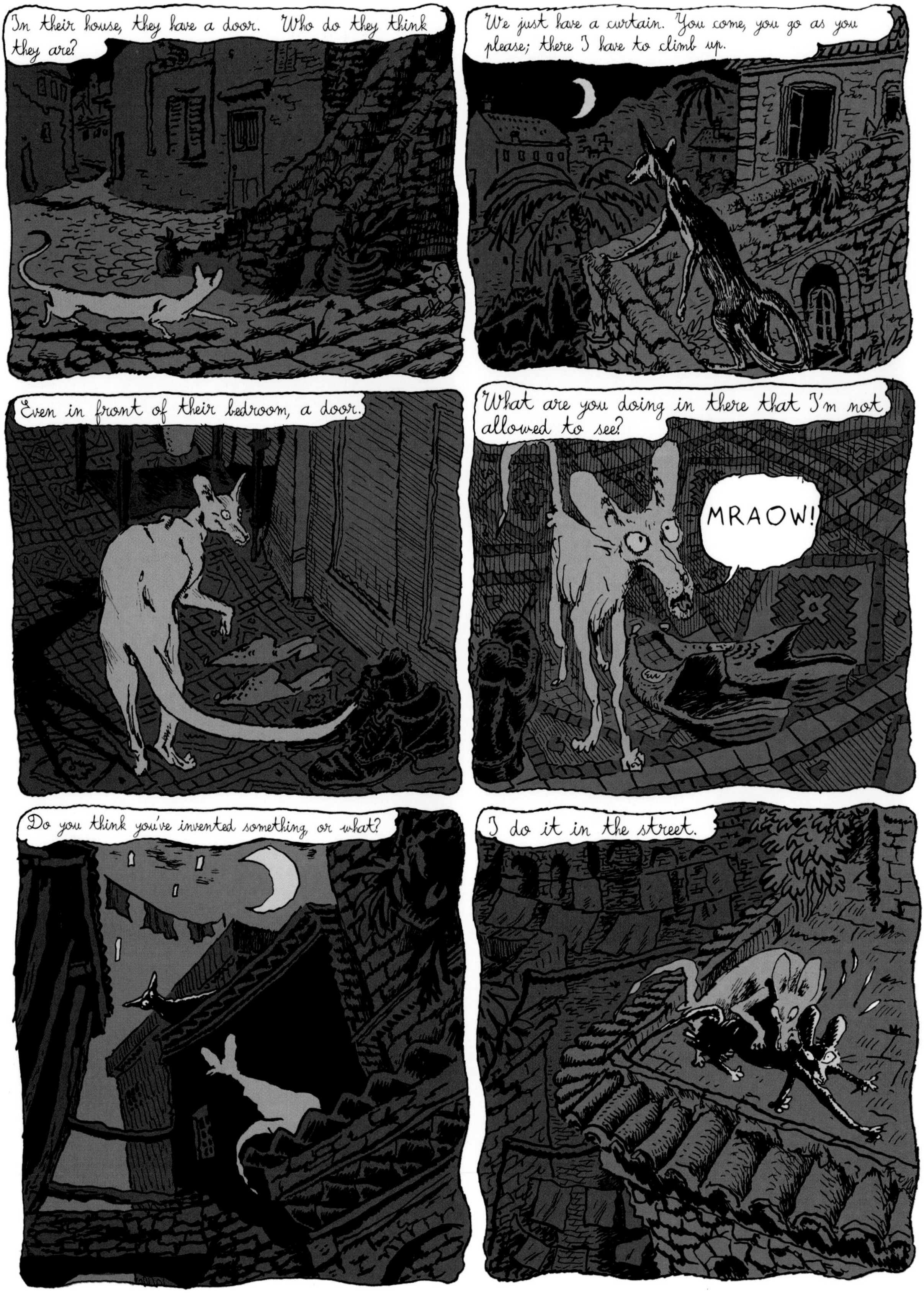
In their house, they have a door. Who do they think they are?
We just have a curtain. You come, you go as you please; there I have to climb up.
Even in front of their bedroom, a door.
What are you doing in there that I'm not allowed to see?
MRAOW!
Do you think you've invented something or what?
I do it in the street.

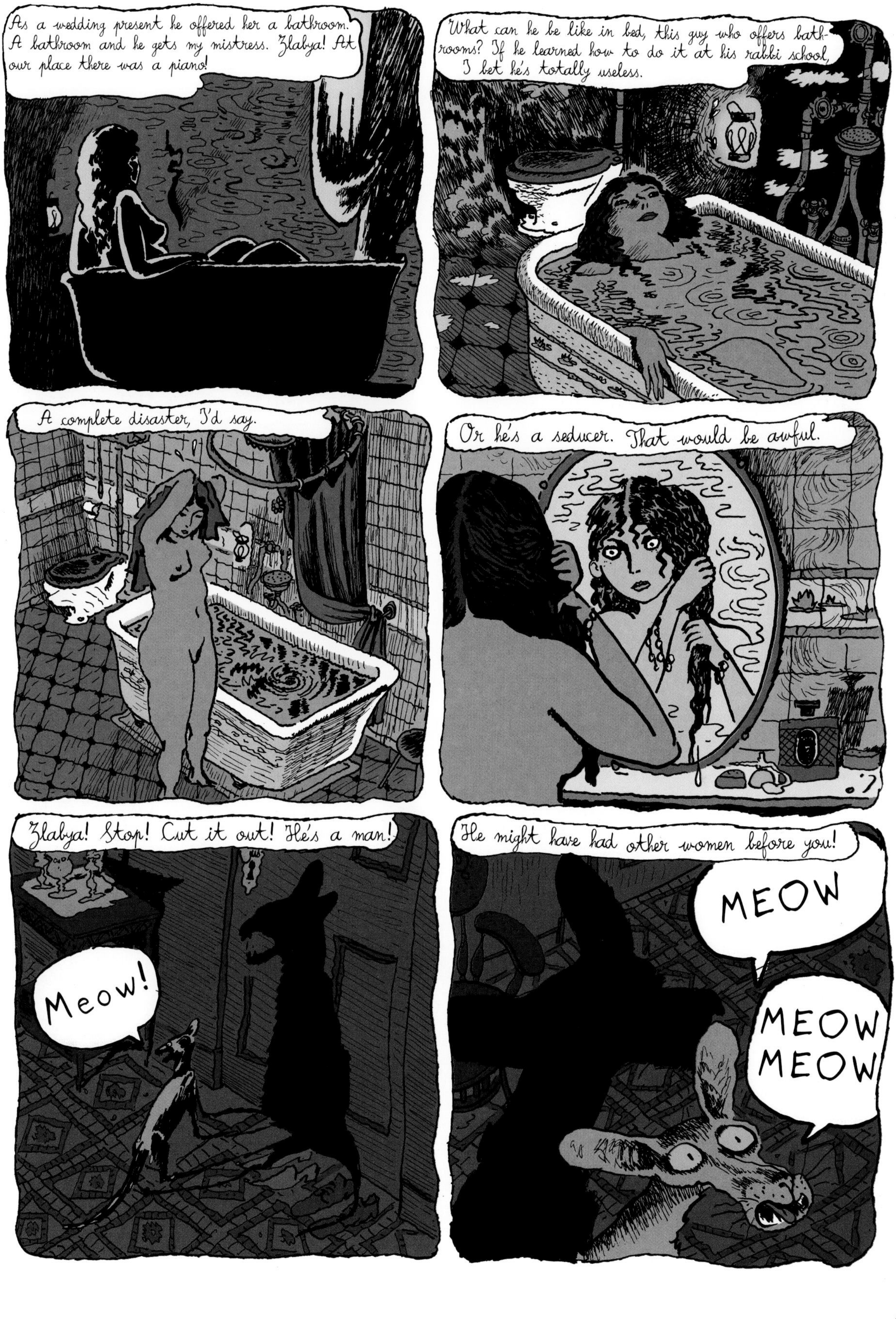
As a wedding present he offered her a bathroom. A bathroom and he gets my mistress. Zlabya! At our place there was a piano!
What can he be like in bed, this guy who offers bathrooms? If he learned how to do it at his rabbi school, I bet he's totally useless.
A complete disaster, I'd say.
Or he's a seducer. That would be awful.
Zlabya! Stop! Cut it out! He's a man!
Meow!
He might have had other women before you!
MEOW
MEOW MEOW

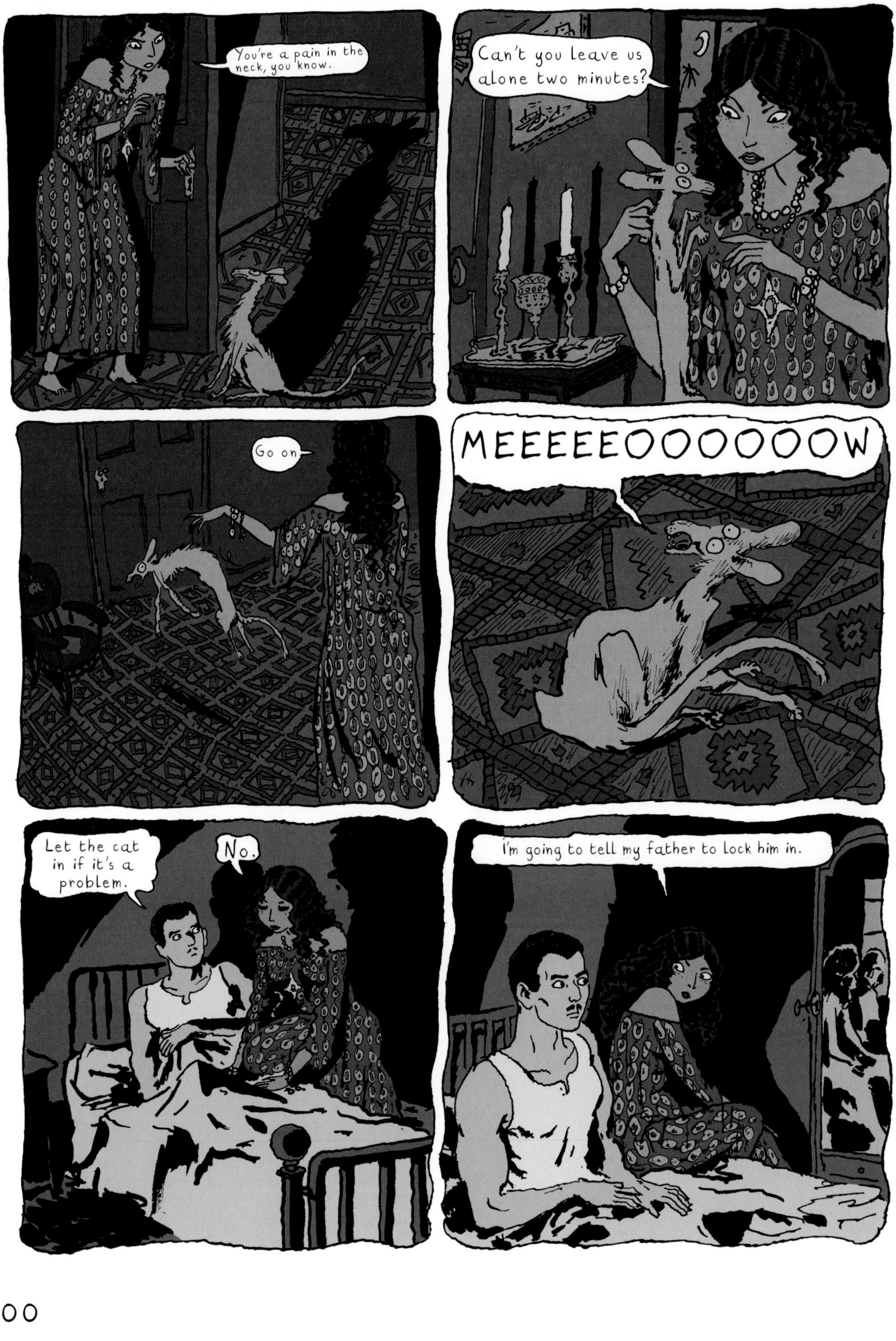
You're a pain in the neck, you know.
Can't you leave us alone two minutes?
Go on
MEEEEEOOOOOOW
Let the cat in if it's a problem.
No.
I'm going to tell my father to lock him in.

The young man's father didn't even come to the wedding. So for their honeymoon they're going to see him in Paris.

When my master said we were going to accompany them, I think they were less than thrilled.

But my master grumbled, so they got him a ticket. I ride for free.

Don't you think it's important that I get to know my son-in-law's family?

Of course it is, Dad.

Zlabya filled her biggest suitcase because she wants to be beautiful in Paris. My master also brought a trunk filled with books, and the young man gets to lug it all.

When the boat sets off, my master pulls a bit of a number.

Why are you crying?

Because we're leaving Algeria.

It's my first time crossing the sea.

Give me a break! In ten days we'll be on the boat coming back.

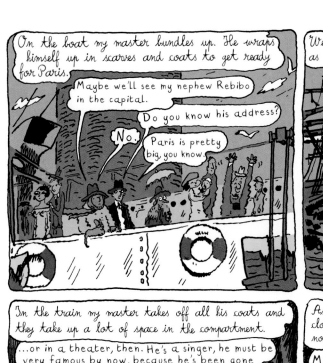

On the boat my master bundles up. He wraps himself up in scarves and coats to get ready for Paris.

Maybe we'll see my nephew Rebibo in the capital.

Do you know his address?

No.

Paris is pretty big, you know.

We arrive in Marseille and it's just as warm as at home.

Well, if we go to the synagogue we're sure to bump into him.

Dad, there are tons of synagogues in Paris.

Oh, so now you're the expert on Paris synagogues?

BIERE PHENIX

BAR DE LA DÉGUSTATION MARSEILL

Search up and down, roaming each hemisphere...

...ain't no place as nice as our Marseille here...

In the train my master takes off all his coats and they take up a lot of space in the compartment.

...or in a theater, then. He's a singer, he must be very famous by now, because he's been gone for...Ooooh, let's see, how long has it been? ...three years. Doesn't the name Raymond Rebibo ring a bell, son?

No.

As the train pulls into Avignon, my master sees a cloud and tells us that we're entering the northern part of France.

Maybe he sings under another name.

What, Raymond Rebibo would renounce his ancestors' name? Cut it out, will you?

He puts his warm clothes back on and is going to keep them on until Paris.

In any case, I wonder what's become of him. We've had no news since he moved to Paris.

Maybe he was ashamed.

Of what?

By the time we get off the train at Gare de Lyon in Paris the rabbi's all sweaty. At the first draft of cold air he starts to sneeze.

I don't know, maybe things didn't work out with his career and until he makes it big he prefers to lie low.

Oh, no. You'll hear how he sings. He can even do opera. And he dresses up. He tells jokes all the time.

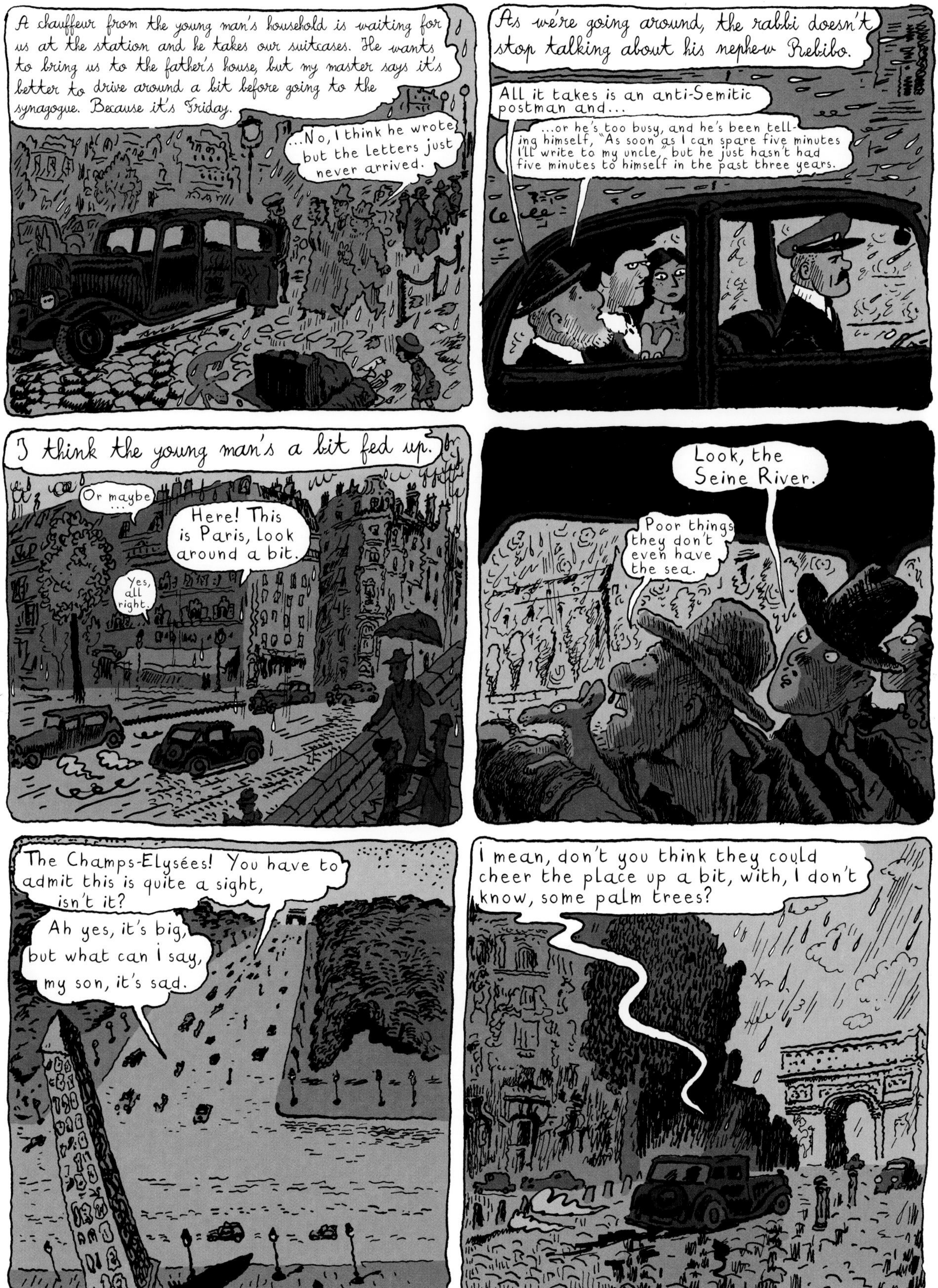
A chauffeur from the young man's household is waiting for us at the station and he takes our suitcases. He wants to bring us to the father's house, but my master says it's better to drive around a bit before going to the synagogue. Because it's Friday.
...No, I think he wrote but the letters just never arrived.
As we're going around, the rabbi doesn't stop talking about his nephew Rebibo.
All it takes is an anti-Semitic postman and...
...or he's too busy, and he's been telling himself, "As soon as I can spare five minutes I'll write to my uncle," but he just hasn't had five minutes to himself in the past three years.
I think the young man's a bit fed up.
Or maybe...
Here! This is Paris, look around a bit.
Yes, all right.
Look, the Seine River.
Poor things they don't even have the sea.
The Champs-Elysées! You have to admit this is quite a sight, isn't it?
Ah yes, it's big, but what can I say, my son, it's sad.
I mean, don't you think they could cheer the place up a bit, with, I don't know, some palm trees?

Really, the poor things. Luckily they're busy all the time, because in this city if you have two minutes to sit down and look up at the sky, it makes you cry it's so gray.

What?

Why are you giving your old father that black look, that makes you look like Pharaoh cursing Moshe Rabbenu?

If you didn't want your father around in Paris, you should have said so, Zlabya.

BAR LA BENAI

Do you think this is making me happy, this exodus? Do you imagine I'm pleased to see my daughter's husband take her to the land of Eskimos?

Dad, Daaad, it's Shabbat!

We're going to the synagogue, then we'll have dinner with Jules's parents, and after that we're having a good holiday. And if afterward you don't want to go out, if you want to spend a whole week in your room, grumbling and awaiting the return, you go right ahead.

You want to lock me up now? She's ashamed of me!

FERRO N L

I've never seen my master like this. I'm delighted. We go to the synagogue. My master finds it very beautiful but he doesn't say so.

Good evening, Mr. Melloul.

Good evening, son.

Shuvi, shuvi, hashu-lamit, shuvi, shuvi, veterezena.

He tries to open a drawer to take a prayer book but can't. A member of the congregation explains that they only open with a key.

What are you afraid of? You think someone's going to steal a book from the synagogue?

Hey, even with the drawers locked it's already happened.

Lecha dodi likrat kala penei shabaaat.

Listen a little to the prayers.

My master explains that where we come from it's not like that, and he says it's a sad state of affairs. The people in front ask him to be quiet, they can't hear themselves praying.

Veshameru bene Yisrael et hashabbat.

Vrooooooom.

My master gets angry and says that he's a rabbi and that where we come from, in Algeria, we're smart enough to talk while praying and that if in Paris they only know how to do one thing at a time, M'ksina, he feels sorry for them.

Vrooom.

That is to say, my son, here they pray seriously. I mean, listen to this silence. There's an echo, you'd think you were in a church. Back home, for Shabbat, we sing. Tell them to really sing.

Igdal elohim chai ve ich-taabar...

Nimsach vehen et el messi-huto...

Vraaaow Rat-tat-tat Boom

From upstairs—because the women pray upstairs—Zlabya watches her husband yelling at her father. And I look at Zlabya and wonder what the hell we're doing here.

After the synagogue, the chauffeur comes to pick us up, but my master says that on Shabbat we have to walk home.

And we didn't see your father at the synagogue, son.

He's not very religious.

In Algeria, too, we walk everywhere on Shabbat, only there it doesn't rain.

Okay, he's not very religious, fine, but, I mean, this is Shabbat.

He doesn't do Shabbat too much.

Too much? Does he or doesn't he?

Doesn't.

Chas ve'shalom! My daughter, you're bringing me to the home of people who don't fear God.

Everything will be strictly kosher, I made sure of it.

Yes.

But sleeping there, I just can't do that. Not in a house where they'll be switching lights on, switching them off, switching them back on again, carrying things, maybe even smoking. You take me to a hotel, my daughter.

But what are you going to pay with, seeing that it's Shabbat and we're not supposed to touch money tonight!

Daaaad!

Tomorrow evening, I'll pay them. Find me a hotel, Zlabya.

Please! Don't do this to me. It's an insult to my father!

It's just too serious.

What? You're going to come, eat, and then you'll get up and say "I'm going to sleep at the hotel"?

No, not like that, you can't.

Come along now.

106

What? He rings the doorbell on Shabbat! What sort of rabbi is he, this one?

RiiiiiiNG!

No, wait!

I'm going to go. You'll say I stayed in Algiers, that I missed the boat.

You're crazy!

You'll say that it's your honeymoon, and you weren't going to burden yourselves with an old man. I'm leaving. Be sure to give a big hug to your parents, my son.

But Dad! Where are you going to go?

We'll meet up at the train station. In a week's time.

But he doesn't even have his things. He has no money.

Let him go. He's pissing me off.

And me, what am I supposed to do? Should I stay in this house of Jews who are so elegant you'd swear they were French, with the beautiful rugs and the smell of fine cooking, or follow my master in the rain?

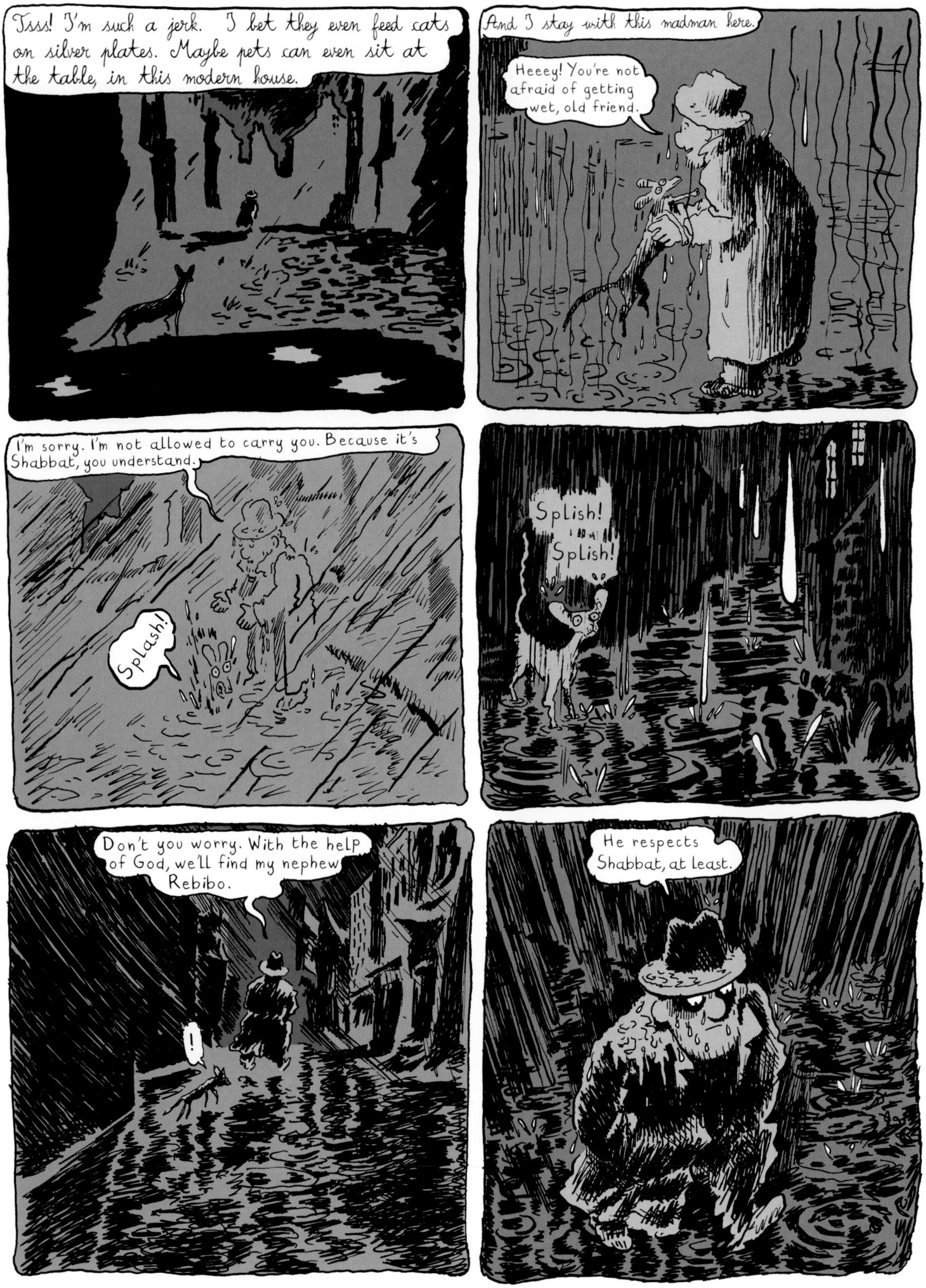
Tsss! I'm such a jerk. I bet they even feed cats on silver plates. Maybe pets can even sit at the table, in this modern house.
And I stay with this madman here.
Heeey! You're not afraid of getting wet, old friend.
I'm sorry. I'm not allowed to carry you. Because it's Shabbat, you understand.
Splash!
Splish!
Splish!
Don't you worry. With the help of God, we'll find my nephew Rebibo.
!
He respects Shabbat, at least.

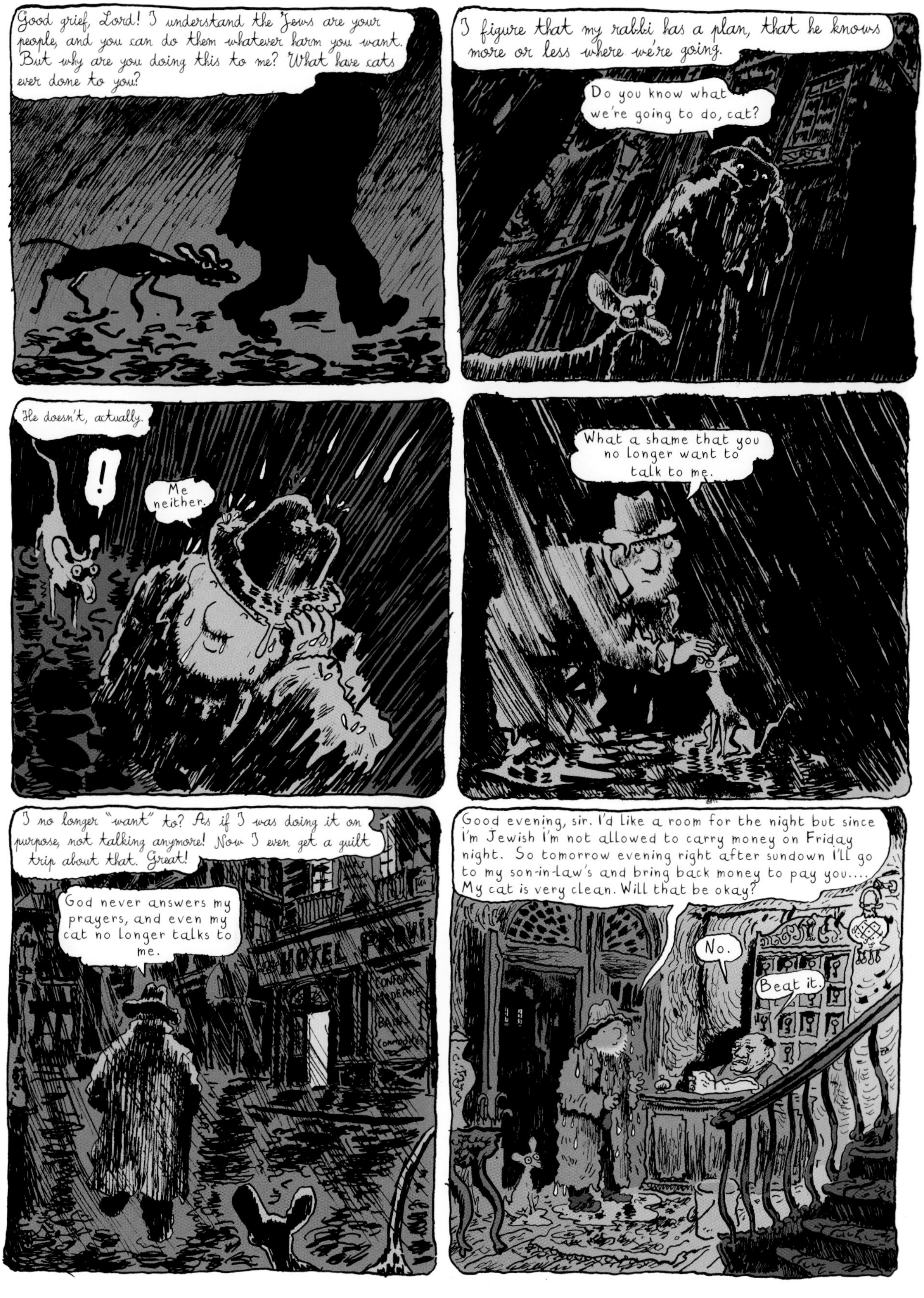

Good grief, Lord! I understand the Jews are your people, and you can do them whatever harm you want. But why are you doing this to me? What have cats ever done to you?
I figure that my rabbi has a plan, that he knows more or less where we're going.
Do you know what we're going to do, cat?
He doesn't, actually.
!
Me neither.
What a shame that you no longer want to talk to me.
I no longer "want" to? As if I was doing it on purpose, not talking anymore! Now I even get a guilt trip about that. Great!
God never answers my prayers, and even my cat no longer talks to me.
HOTEL
Good evening, sir. I'd like a room for the night but since I'm Jewish I'm not allowed to carry money on Friday night. So tomorrow evening right after sundown I'll go to my son-in-law's and bring back money to pay you.... My cat is very clean. Will that be okay?
No.
Beat it.

(Tch! You couldn't shut up, could you? You could've just gone to sleep and told your life story tomorrow morning.)

Meow! Meow!

Stop the meowing. Speak or be quiet.

He said we were going for a walk. Then he sneezed and his nose started running. Because all his handkerchiefs were in the suitcase, he wiped his nose with his sleeve and it was disgusting. He finally suggested that we go sleep in the synagogue.

But it was closed and there was an electric doorbell. My master did not want to violate the Shabbat by using an electrical device. So we trudged off in the rain like idiots.

A bit farther we saw a small church. It was open. Is there a commandment that forbids us from entering a church?

No. God is everywhere, and here it isn't raining.

I hope we won't get kicked out if someone finds us.

Meow! (Of course not, dummy!)

There's no one but us in the church, but my master still wants to respect their ways: Christians take their hats off in church. But in our tradition, you're not allowed to go before your Creator with your head uncovered.

I'll take off my hat but keep my skullcap.

My master isn't very comfortable in front of this rabbi from Palestine dying on the cross.

> How can they concentrate on their prayers in front of this sculpture? You even see the blood and the eyes rolled back in pain. How am I going to fall asleep in front of this?

And in these boxes? Bones! They display pieces of the corpses of their great men.

> Meow! (Maybe they buried the person and afterward found a missing piece, so they put it in the box in the meantime.)

On the other side, you can see a painting of a young woman whose eyes have been stabbed, another who had molten lead poured down her throat, and one with severed breasts that she's carrying on a tray. My master is terrified.

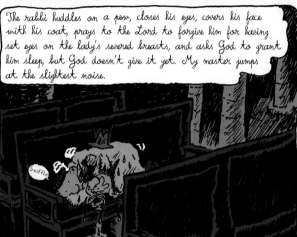

The rabbi huddles on a pew, closes his eyes, covers his face with his coat, prays to the Lord to forgive him for having set eyes on the lady's severed breasts, and asks God to grant him sleep, but God doesn't give it yet. My master jumps at the slightest noise.

Sniffle

Tap! Tap! Tap! The quick footfalls of a creature of God coming, like us, to seek shelter from the rain. The rabbi gets ready to clear out and apologize for being there and for being Jewish and for having looked at the naked lady and the bleeding idol and for abusing their hospitality, and also for Pontius Pilate who killed the rabbi from Palestine, with the consequences that we all know.

But the creature is only one of those little dogs that they have in Paris, so it is fine.

> Woof! (Hi there, bums!)

111

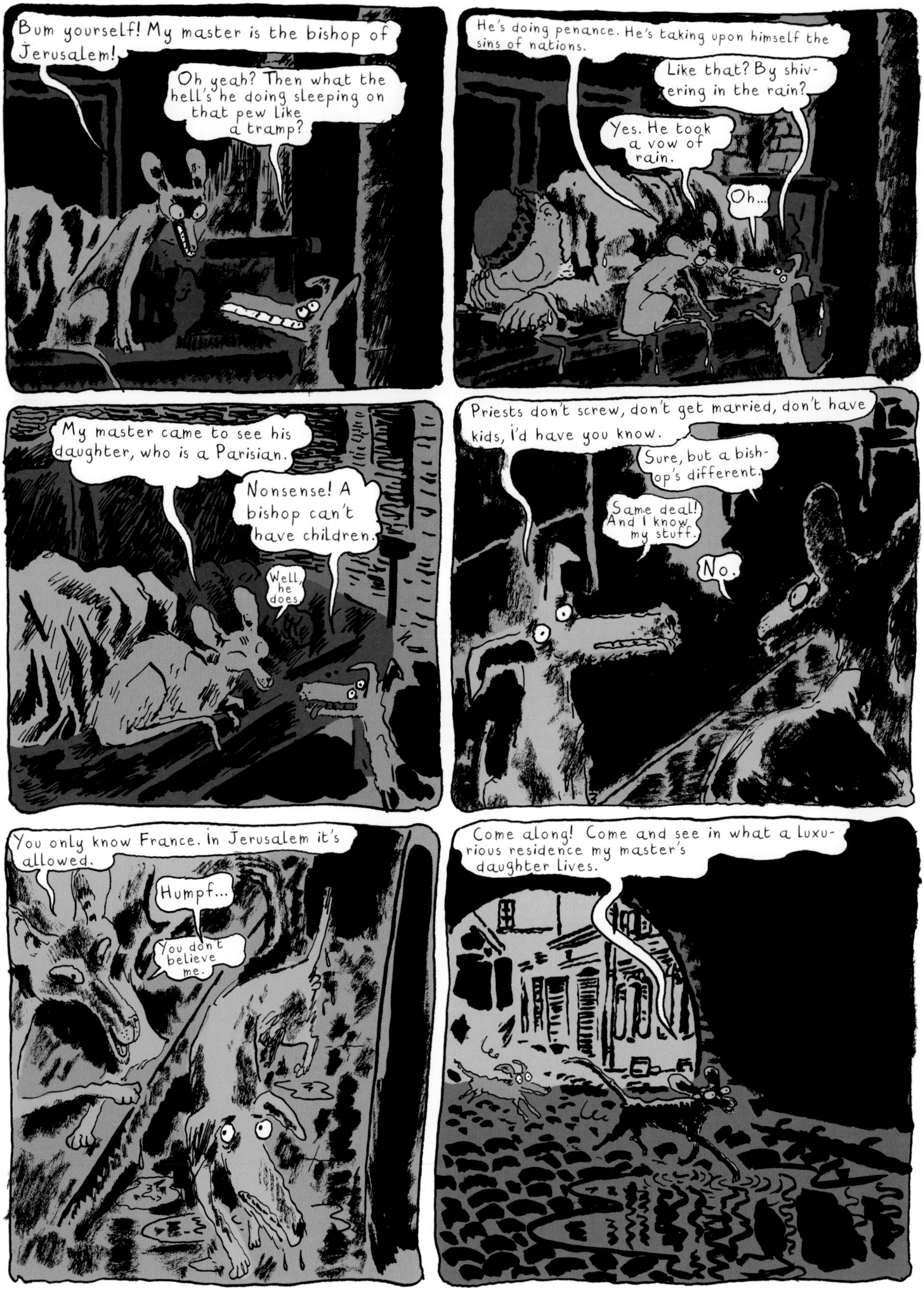
Bum yourself! My master is the bishop of Jerusalem!
Oh yeah? Then what the hell's he doing sleeping on that pew like a tramp?
He's doing penance. He's taking upon himself the sins of nations.
Like that? By shivering in the rain?
Yes. He took a vow of rain.
Oh...
My master came to see his daughter, who is a Parisian.
Nonsense! A bishop can't have children.
Well, he does.
Priests don't screw, don't get married, don't have kids, I'd have you know.
Sure, but a bishop's different.
Same deal! And I know my stuff.
No.
You only know France. In Jerusalem it's allowed.
Humpf...
You don't believe me.
Come along! Come and see in what a luxurious residence my master's daughter lives.

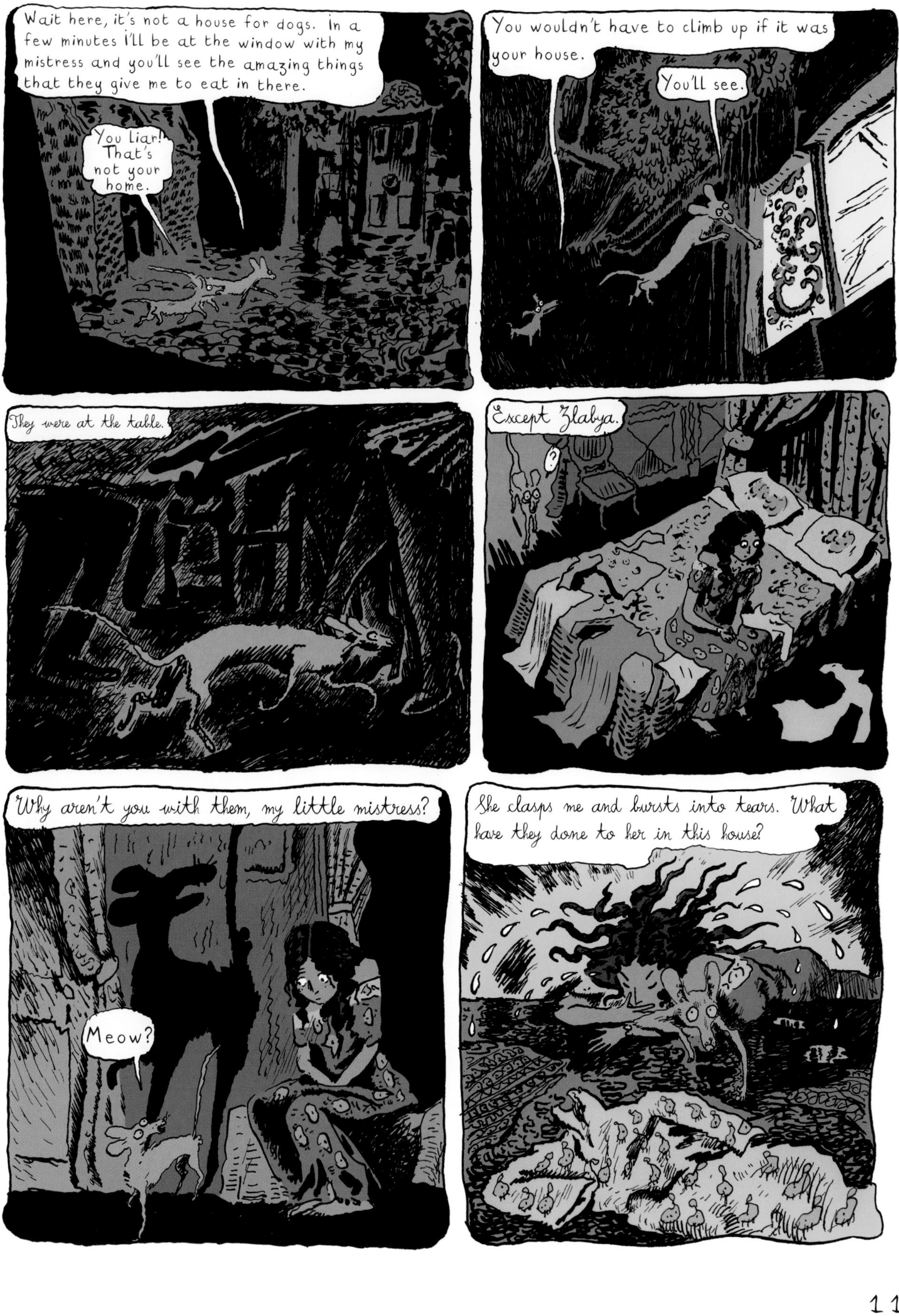
Wait here, it's not a house for dogs. In a few minutes I'll be at the window with my mistress and you'll see the amazing things that they give me to eat in there.
You liar! That's not your home.
You wouldn't have to climb up if it was your house.
You'll see.
They were at the table.
Except Zlabya.
?
Why aren't you with them, my little mistress?
Meow?
She clasps me and bursts into tears. What have they done to her in this house?

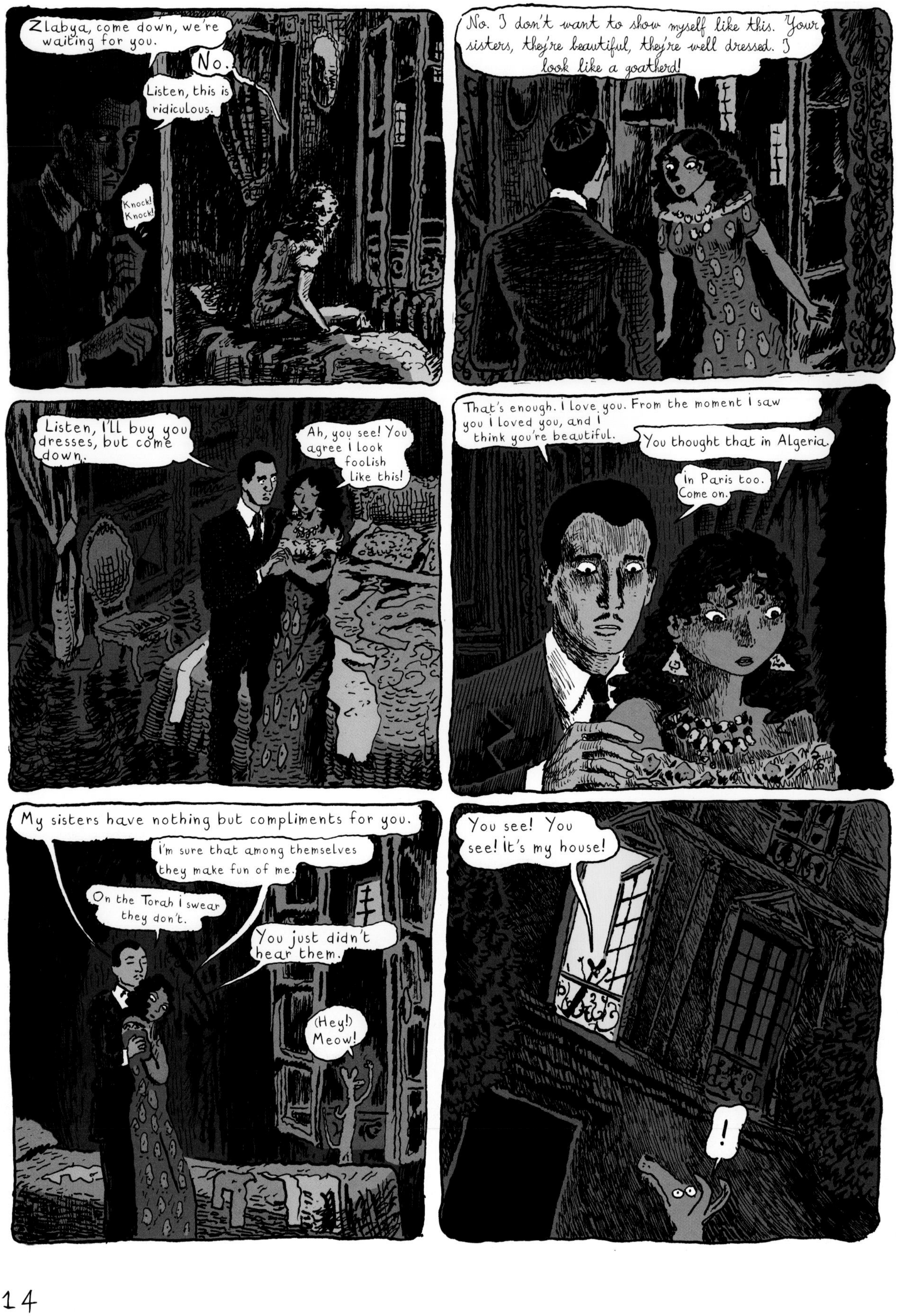
Zlabya, come down, we're waiting for you.
No.
Listen, this is ridiculous.
Knock! Knock!
No. I don't want to show myself like this. Your sisters, they're beautiful, they're well dressed. I look like a goatherd!
Listen, I'll buy you dresses, but come down.
Ah, you see! You agree I look foolish like this!
That's enough. I love you. From the moment I saw you I loved you, and I think you're beautiful.
You thought that in Algeria.
In Paris too. Come on.
My sisters have nothing but compliments for you.
I'm sure that among themselves they make fun of me.
On the Torah I swear they don't.
You just didn't hear them.
(Hey!) Meow!
You see! You see! It's my house!
!

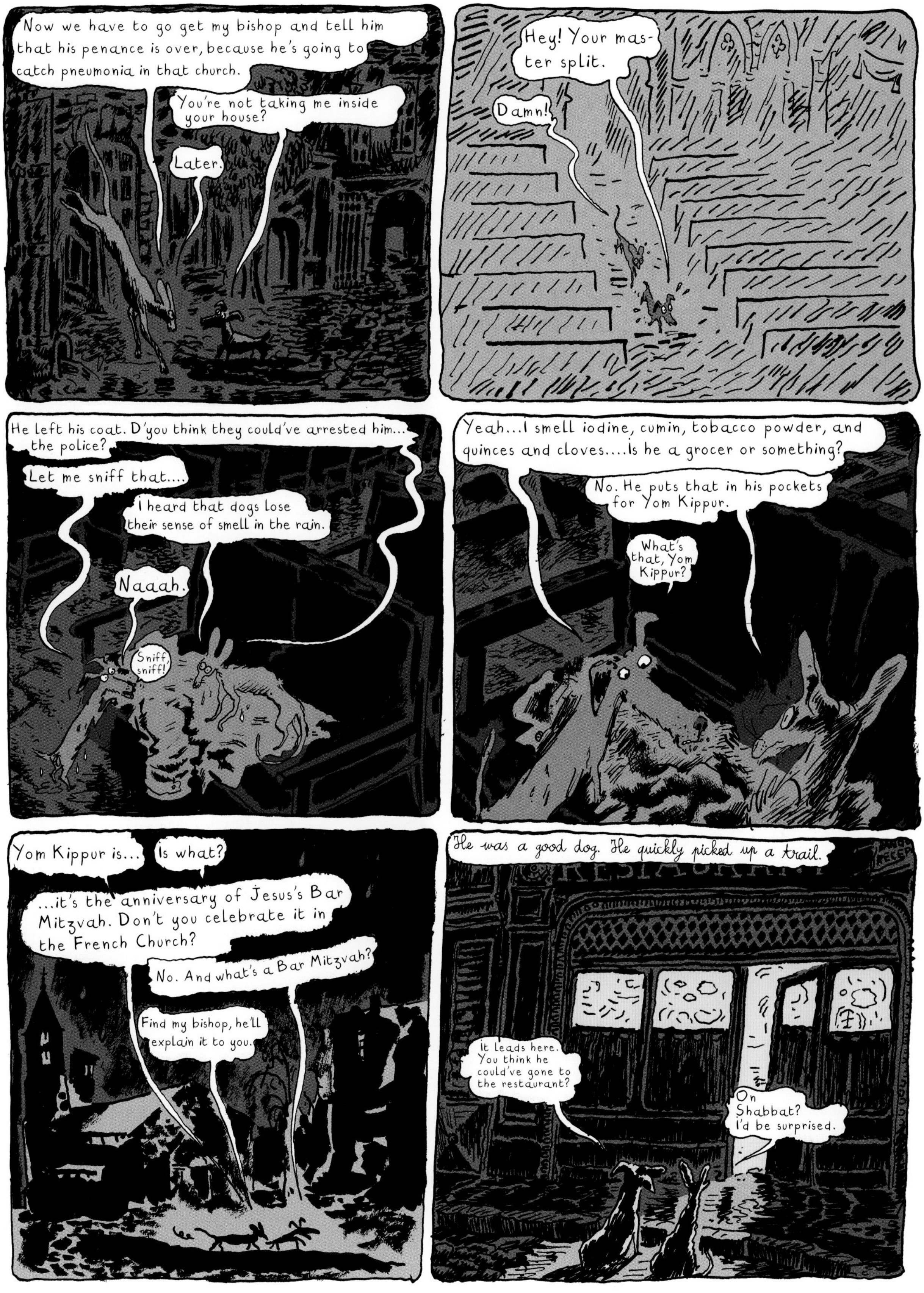
Now we have to go get my bishop and tell him that his penance is over, because he's going to catch pneumonia in that church.
You're not taking me inside your house?
Later.
Hey! Your master split.
Damn!
He left his coat. D'you think they could've arrested him... the police?
Let me sniff that....
I heard that dogs lose their sense of smell in the rain.
Naaah.
Sniff sniff!
Yeah...I smell iodine, cumin, tobacco powder, and quinces and cloves....Is he a grocer or something?
No. He puts that in his pockets for Yom Kippur.
What's that, Yom Kippur?
Yom Kippur is...
Is what?
...it's the anniversary of Jesus's Bar Mitzvah. Don't you celebrate it in the French Church?
No. And what's a Bar Mitzvah?
Find my bishop, he'll explain it to you.
He was a good dog. He quickly picked up a trail.
It leads here. You think he could've gone to the restaurant?
On Shabbat? I'd be surprised.

He was there, alone at a table, and he was ordering.

Well, sir, I have a lot of money to pay you with and I would like to eat well.

Certainly, sir.

I love you.

You say that to all the girls.

No, no.

Do you have ham?

...The subject heading was appealing, but after the introduction the house of cards had toppled.

But of course, how can anyone know how to write before forty?

And blood sausage? That thing made with pig's blood, you serve that to your customers?

Absolutely, sir.

So give me some ham, some blood sausage, snails, seafood, and swordfish, which is a fish without scales, and oysters—and please check that they're really alive. And a glass of milk with the ham. And a good wine named after a church or a Virgin Mary.

Châteauneuf-du-Pape?

Perfect.

Hmm...and please make sure that the bottle isn't opened by a Jew and that no Jew says any prayer over this food.

I'll make sure, sir.

What does your bishop have against Jews?

Here you are, you two.

You're going to witness the least kosher meal in the universe.

Careful, the plate is hot.

Slurp!

Wag! Wag!

Kiss.

The little dog wants some, too; here, boy....Lord, talk to me. Lord, you can see me, I'm about to break your commandments. Tell me not to do it.

Tell me that I've deprived myself of these foods for sixty years and that it served some kind of purpose. Tell me you'll be sad if I break your Law.

Tell me that when my wife died it was your will and it was a part of your design....He says nothing....He's testing me.

Or he doesn't exist. Or he belongs only to the sphere of being, which amounts to the same thing.

The rabbi eats and the world doesn't fall apart.

Just this once, I'll have eaten all this, Lord. Tomorrow I'll go back to fearing you.

Blessed are you, Lord our God, who allow us to transgress.*

*Blessing for non-kosher food.

Tell me something, Mr. Waiter. I'm going to pay you because I have a lot of money on me, but first, can you tell me what you do in Paris when you're looking for a gentleman called Rebibo and you don't know his address?

If he has a telephone, one can look in the telephone book, sir.

Ah, that's good.

In Algiers too we have a telephone book. But there's no phone in my house.... Hmm, let's see.... Oh, I'm not familiar with this telephone book. Would you mind looking up Rebibo for me, because without my glasses...

Very well, sir.

Rebibo, Raymond?

That's him! Please call him, O great reader of telephone books in French!

He reached his nephew, who told him all was well and that he was a musical performer in a theater. The rabbi asked him if he was rich and Rebibo said that, thank heaven, he was doing all right. So the rabbi asked him to come and join us to pay for the restaurant.

There, that's settled. The singer Raymond Rebibo will come in person to your establishment, and he's going to pay you.

We're going to wait for him.

After a long while, the nephew Rebibo finally got there.

Hey, Uncle!

El Rebibo! You're the best, son! You're so handsome! Come here, let me bless ya!

Clap! Clap! Clap!

He paid the restaurant, and we all left together.

Why are you carrying a bag on Shabbat, son?

That's my stage costume, Uncle.

Because you're doing your laundry on a Friday night?

No, Uncle.

The priests I know say "Father" and "My son," but he says "Uncle"?

Yes

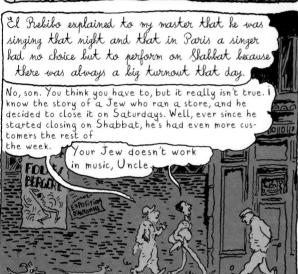

El Rebibo explained to my master that he was singing that night and that in Paris a singer had no choice but to perform on Shabbat because there was always a big turnout that day.

No, son. You think you have to, but it really isn't true. I know the story of a Jew who ran a store, and he decided to close it on Saturdays. Well, ever since he started closing on Shabbat, he's had even more customers the rest of the week.

Your Jew doesn't work in music, Uncle.

FOLIES BERGÈRE

EXPOSITION D'AUTOMNE

Uncle, I don't want you to have to witness a guy breaking Shabbat. So I'll drop you off at my place and then I'll go sing.

No, I want to hear you. I'm proud of you.

BAR

You think I could be ashamed of you because you break one of God's commandments? One commandment out of six hundred and thirteen and I should deprive myself of the pleasure of hearing my little Raymond sing? Who held you on his lap on the day of your circumcision? Who gave you your first cigarette for your Bar Mitzvah? My Raymond, he's singing in Paris and I'm not going to go see him? Come on! What's it called, your theater?

Le Grand Guignol, Uncle.

I don't know that one. It's kind of a comedy theater, right?

Uncle, it's not a good idea for you to come.

Why? There are naked women, is that it?

No...

So I'm coming.

Wow, this year the banks of the Seine are always flooded.

119

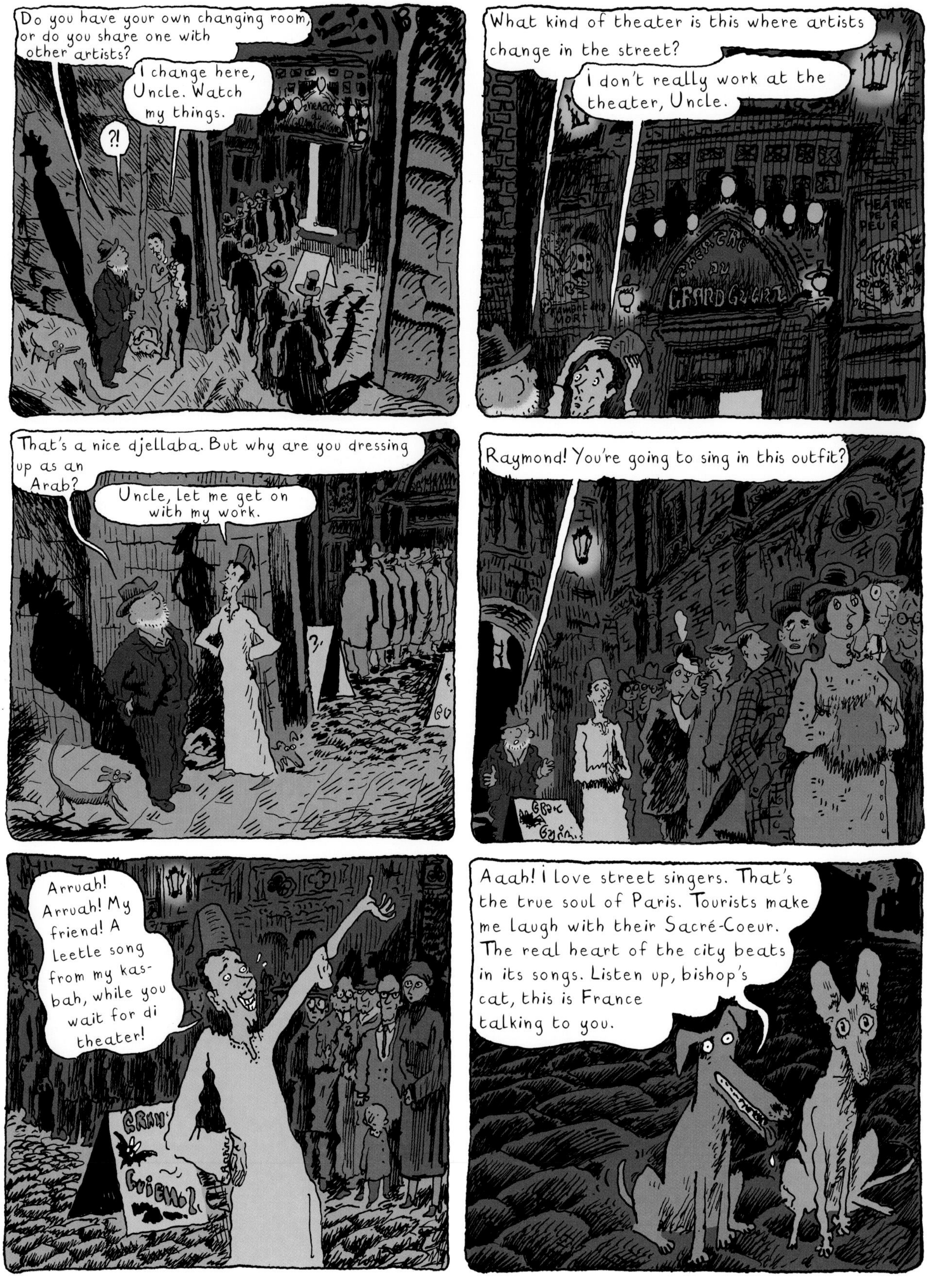
Do you have your own changing room, or do you share one with other artists?
I change here, Uncle. Watch my things.
?!
What kind of theater is this where artists change in the street?
I don't really work at the theater, Uncle.
That's a nice djellaba. But why are you dressing up as an Arab?
Uncle, let me get on with my work.
?!
Raymond! You're going to sing in this outfit?
Arruah! Arruah! My friend! A leetle song from my kasbah, while you wait for di theater!
Aaah! I love street singers. That's the true soul of Paris. Tourists make me laugh with their Sacré-Coeur. The real heart of the city beats in its songs. Listen up, bishop's cat, this is France talking to you.

loosely adapted from "Arrouah, j't'y cire" (Aïssa/Diodat/R. Desmoulins), Buda musique no. 82966-2. "Algeria-Humorous songwriters of the 1930s"

121

My master is in shock.

The people are happy. They give money.

Ha! Ha! Excellent!

There! I made at least fifteen francs.

...

Cling!

Cling!

That's your career?

No, I'm trying to write for a female singer, but that's tough. This works better.

Like this, on the street?

Well, yeah.

But why do you pretend to be an Arab?

Because to play a Jew you have to have a Polish accent, and I don't know how to do it. Playing a North African Jew just doesn't work, people aren't interested, it's too complicated for them.

The public, Uncle, doesn't like things that are complicated.

What did he mean, your dad, when he said, "In Turkey, people would love you."

It was a compliment.

He comes from Turkey. He's Turkish. He lived over there for thirty years. He made a lot of money over there. He met his first wife over there. Everything he likes is Turkish, so when he says you look Turkish, yes, that's a compliment.

Ah.

...

What now?

Nothing.

It's just that, evidently, no one thinks I look like a Parisian.

♥

But answer me, instead of clowning around! If you passed me on the street, would you think, "This one's from Paris"? Or...

kiss

If I bumped into you, I'd lift you up on my Parisian horse and marry you, and if you were already married I'd kill your husband and then you'd let me read my newspaper.

Are you sure I can come, I won't be in the way?

Hey, I don't even know where we're going, so...

I mean, if there are other clergymen...

Enough with that, okay?

You live on this street, son? ... You don't have any more bad news up your sleeve, Raymond?

No, Uncle. We live on this street because it's cheaper, that's all. I'm not a pimp and my girlfriend isn't a hooker.

She is Catholic, though.

You...you...and is it serious, you and this young woman?

Oh, listen, Uncle, with all due respect, shut up.

No, I'm sorry. Let me put it this way, man to man: I'm madly in love with her, but since she's a singer she's banging half of Paris in addition to me. So when she doesn't come home at night I get drunk and if it goes on much longer I'll end up blowing my brains out.

Ah.

My master lets out a sigh of relief.

So there hasn't really been any talk of marriage yet, right?

124

* Moses Maimonides, *The Book of Knowledge*

The nephew wanted to give his bed to the rabbi, but the rabbi insisted on sleeping on the couch.

You know what this apartment needs?

What?

A dog.

Musicians like to surround themselves with small animals; it gives them an outlet for their surfeit of tenderness. I think I'm going to stay here.

Be quiet, someone's coming.

It was the singer. Completely drunk. She didn't even see the dog in her way; she gave him a kick without noticing. But that didn't wake anybody up.

They called him the talent scout....You could say his heart was stout....

La la la

Yelp!

She collapsed in a heap and started snoring while her champagne bottle emptied itself onto the carpet.

Burp!

Wow, she's a helluva lot older than he is, wouldn't you say?

Still, I liked her smell. She had arms like a mom, which dangled a bit. I stretched out alongside her. She liked that.

This kind of woman generally prefers cats to dogs. That's just my luck, because I like women like her.

She must be a great artist.

When the rabbi woke up, he found the little dog curled in his arms.

Hey, aren't you getting a little too familiar?

He loved this apartment. Probably because of the musical instruments.

Meow! (Tell me, did you go into the rabbi business because you couldn't make it in music?)

Be quiet, you! Can't you see there's a lady sleeping?

In the kitchen the rabbi found an old banjo without strings. He put it on his knees and slowly started to beat a rhythm on the taut skin, as if it were a tarbukah.

Meow! (Answer me, you old bird. Rabbi wasn't your calling, was it? You'd have preferred to be a musician.)

Tum, tum, tum

Woof! (Hey, that's not bad.)

El Rebibo arrived. He heated up some coffee and soon sat down next to the rabbi.

What's that, a mandola, a qanun?

No, Uncle, it's a bouzouki. A Greek guy gave it to me when he left.

Can you play Maalouf with it?

Of course.

Did you see, he's a lefty.

So they played together. El Rebibo could have earned the title of sheikh, he played with such ease. He played without seeming to care a damn. But these traditional tunes that seemed joyful to us in Algeria somehow sounded different here.

Maybe it was just the lousy weather, but hearing this in Paris, it was heartbreaking.

You know, man, I'm no tenderheart, but hearing this music just makes me melt.

127

The singer woke up. She didn't seem to mind that there was a cat, a dog, and a rabbi in her apartment. We were in a hospitable home.

You know, for once this isn't bad, sweetie. Did you snort something or could you play again like that in front of an impresario?

You bet I could!

Madam, Raymond here, he's been playing this music since he could walk. Back home, we didn't call him just Rebibo, he was El Rebibo, can you imagine that?

There's an audition at 5 o'clock at Ventura's. You should go, both of you.

The singer scratched me and asked whose dog it was. The rabbi explained that the dog was single.

Yeah, well, if he wants to stay make him take a shower. He stinks.

The rest of the day was taken up with finding a tarbukah and washing the dog.

This one is beautiful, see, there's mother-of-pearl here, and if you remove the skin, it makes a very original vase.

souvenirs ... cadeau
cotillons ... farces ... masque

My master opted for a more modest instrument, but with a nice sound. The salespeople had a great deal of trouble understanding that you could buy an Arab drum to play it and not to decorate your living room.

Can you stop wagging your tail for a minute?

I can't help it; it's the joy of having a master.

Raymond paid for the drum, lent a suit to his uncle, emptied a whole jar of hair lotion on his head, and, three hours before the appointed time, we were waiting in line for the audition.

So what? I love my master, too, it doesn't mean I have to act like an electric fan.

You're not a dog, you can't understand.

It's at about that time that it started to rain.

Don't worry, if they like North African music, they'll love our act.

The two men didn't even realize it was raining because they were dreaming of their music, and the dog was happy because he had a master.

People like what's authentic. If you introduce them to real Algerian music, they can only love it.

I was in a hurry for someone to open the theater.

Can't you just see it, your name up there in big letters, flashing: "Raymond Rebibo, North African Bouzouki"?

God willing, Uncle.

Many artists came to crowd around us before the doorkeeper made up his mind to let us in.

Fortunately, the sight of the rain ruining in pizzicato the opera singers' hairdos, fur coats, and general appearance shortened the wait for me. Finally, someone opened the door.

And by a mechanical process whose cause still escapes me, we who had gotten there first somehow found ourselves practically last in line.

Don't worry, the line moves fast.

Stop wagging your tail.

Waiting in that theater wasn't all that pleasant an experience. The artists were nervous and quarreled for the slightest things. Some had brought animals that weren't as well trained as they should have been.

A guy was walking around with a baboon that decided it was a good idea to devour two doves belonging to a magician.

Thanks to the scuffle caused by this unforeseen voracity, I was able to pounce on a mynah, the only bird who had escaped the carnage.

I carried the bird behind a curtain to finish it off. The meat was nothing to write home about, but I saw an opportunity to recover speech.

Something told me that a talking cat could prove rather useful in the very near future.

At last our turn came.

The welcome wasn't overly effusive.

They did their best while the dog wagged his tail stupidly, all the while giving Mr. Ventura pleading looks.

And in the middle of a particularly haunting section...

As the dog finally stopped wagging his tail like a metronome, my master had an idea.

131

He shook me as much as he could.

Speak.

I tried my best, I really did.

MRAOW!

But I couldn't talk anymore. Maybe the mynah I had swallowed didn't have the gift of speech either. The more I tried, the more I meowed.

Mraow! Mraow! Mraow!

Stop! Stop!

The dog thought he should intervene.

WOOF!

He showed us all the tricks he knew. Standing on his hind legs, up on his front legs, wiggling his ears, dancing on his hind legs. It was pathetic.

Sorry. I never take dog acts, they bore the hell out of everyone.

If you don't mind, I'd like to show you one last thing.

O Sidi Bel Abbes, O my lovely country, from my home Algeria I came to gay Paree, with my shoe-shine box under my arm... Hanana, arruah! Hanana, arruah!

And to earn my living I polish without complaining. Arruah! Arruah! Pretty ma'am, full of charm, is there anything I can shine for you? A little dough is all it'll cost—it's true.

Polish, polish, I do it so fine.

Now that's more like it.

I'm not finished.

It's okay, I've heard enough.

Moniiiique.

Take this young man here, get him an Arab costume, and then ask the props guy for a wooden box, you know, the kind for shining shoes. He starts tomorrow.

Okay, tomorrow 6 p.m. If you're late, you're fired. I pay thirty francs a night if the audience claps, and if not, you're out. Write me a dozen songs in that vein and your fortune's made, my friend.

133

You should accept this job, son. In this line of work, it's hard to break through.

Of course, Uncle. We live in an imperfect world. It's in the afterlife that all is well. Come on, I'll buy you dinner.

No, I have an appointment with my in-laws.

All right, son, till the next time.

Bye, Uncle Abraham.

Take care.

See ya.

We walked ten yards, then the rabbi ran back to his nephew and made him swear that he didn't have anything bad in mind when he said that all would be well in the afterlife. The nephew said he didn't, and that he wasn't an idealist, and that if he ever killed himself one day it would be over a woman and certainly not because of work. So my master was reassured and we left for good.

134

Jules, can you stop walking around like a shoplifter?

What do you expect?

You take me shopping on a Saturday afternoon and you want me to act normal. I'm a rabbi! If people recognize me, what will they think?

I thought you were accountable only to God?

Yes, yes.

And if Jews see you here, it means they too are breaking Shabbat.

You know very well that it's different for a rabbi.

Do you like this?

For a cleric's wife, it's a little indecent, no?

Your sister was wearing a shorter one.

God's greatly amused that you're here. He thinks that you're a very nice rabbi, who takes good care of his wife.

I'd prefer to hear him tell me so himself.

Jules! I am the Lord your God who brought you out of Egypt and made you cross the Red Sea without getting your pants wet. I command you to buy very pretty dresses for your wife. And shoes.

That makes me feel better.

Shoes with very high heels, because she's short, the poor thing.

When we showed up at the house of the young man's parents, there weren't many people around.

I'm delighted to meet you. I'm the mom.

The kids are out shopping, but my husband is here.

Aarmaaaand! Zlabya's dad is here. Armaaaand! It's awful, he doesn't hear. As soon as he's in his office, nothing else exists.

And this is the famous cat. Let's give him some milk.

Great!

Come on, Armand, look after the gentleman.

Hmm...

Come and see, it's extraordinary.

I'm Zlabya's...

Yes, come and see.

Be good.

I'd been told that they put chocolate in Neptune tobacco, but I didn't believe it; honey, sure, but chocolate! But it's true. Look at these fibers, it's not just a flavoring, is it? It's the plant itself.

Ah...yes...

From now on, I'll be able to smoke with the satisfaction of knowing that I'm eating chocolate at the same time. Would you like some?

I'm waiting to see three stars.

136

Once night has fallen completely, Shabbat will be over and I'll be able to smoke with you.

So it'll be soon.

But I'm allowed to fill my pipe in the meantime.

Please do.

I often do that when the end of Shabbat is near. I roll a cigarette, I finger tobacco.

So now we're part of the same family. I'm glad, you seem like a nice guy.

I cheat on my wife.

That's none of my business.

I haven't set foot in a synagogue for thirty years.

That's very good. That way you don't disturb people during their prayers.

But God has a place for you. Every Shabbat he looks at your empty chair in the synagogue, and he says, "Where is he, this one?" He worries for you. You don't come to services because you want to worry God. You're like the little boy who wants his parents to take better care of him.

I think it's night-time now.

And because he doesn't get hugged, he starts acting up, hoping that at least he'll get a slap. You're doing that to call God.

No.

137

Why are you telling me this? Because I'm a rabbi? I don't know any more than you do. I say my prayers, you don't, what can I tell you? Questions, we all have them. I'm not intelligent enough to respond to your concerns.

Yes, there is one thing that you can teach me.

Ah.

Look, my children were raised like Westerners. We never observed the holidays, never kept kosher, nothing. Not only that, but for their religious instruction I enrolled them in Sunday school.

They're all loving children. They succeed at everything they undertake. They've given me nothing but satisfaction.

Baruch Hashem!

Bless you.

The Jews in our circle look more French than Victor Hugo without the beard. So can you tell me what got into my eldest son's head to make him become a rabbi?

How do you expect me to answer that?

What I mean is, you have to have been through the conditioning, you have to have suffered, you have to be illiterate, or really not understand a thing about life, to want to do something like that! And where does he go for this rabbi business? To Africa!! It took us three hundred years to extricate ourselves from Turkey, and he dives right back into Africa.

North Africa.

Same difference.

I really don't know. Maybe it's the appeal of his maternal grandfather's city. Maybe he had some childhood memories. Maybe he enjoys reading Hebrew. I really can't say anything about it.

Or I could just tell you how I became a rabbi.

You don't come from a religious family?

Not really.

I'm talking about a time when Algerian Jews weren't French yet. Over there, you had the French, the Arabs, the Berbers, and then us at the bottom of the heap. Well, even among us, who were looked down on by everyone else in Algeria, being a rabbi wasn't popular. I remember my poor mother saying, "That's no job for a Jew."

I was in love with a French girl. She liked me too, but she didn't want a Jew for a husband.

Afterward I fell in love with a Jewish girl, but she was rich and her parents didn't want anything to do with me.

You didn't have a good job?

I didn't know how to read. It was the rabbi who was teaching me.

The truth is, you go where people will accept you.

Okay, but what about my son?

I don't know. But perhaps you do?

Me? What can I possibly say? My parents made religion such a pain in the ass that I wanted to spare him that. And what does he do? He dives in headfirst!

He could've had anything. I had prepared everything for him.

And he did something else. He wanted to surprise you.

I too wonder why he's a rabbi, this boy.

Show-off!

It's as if a cat took it into his head to look after the other cats.

In any case, the mother knows how to treat a cat.

RRRRRRRR

Rub! Rub!

Maybe once Zlabya becomes a mother she'll take better care of me.

I gave all my children a little rag doll like that, with an outfit that I knitted myself.

Because since her wedding, she's been doing a lousy job.

Jules must have his somewhere.

Ha! Ha! We'll ask him.

Oh, and that was for a Purim celebration. I had dressed it up as Queen Esther.

But it's a boy!

At the time, everyone dressed them up like that. It didn't matter.

Yeah, well it sure looks silly.

Ah, Zlabya, you have such beautiful hair. Mine used to be like that, too.

I was thinking of maybe getting it cut shorter. I saw in a catalog that people are doing that.

Don't even think of it! Even my youngest daughter who's always up to the minute with the latest fashions said she dreams of wearing her hair long like you do.

Oh, really?

And who's this?

Ah, that's my poor father.

Ah yes, Mr. Corcos.

Zlabya, do you like children?

...er...I don't know.

That's very good.

Ha! Ha! You're lucky your mother-in-law is in Paris! Otherwise you'd always have me underfoot.

Okay!

This is all well and good, but I'd better take advantage of the milk. Once we're back in Algiers, I won't be getting this very often.

Slurp! Slurp!

141

During the return trip, the rabbi was sad because he missed Paris.

Morai VeRabotai, dear friends, I met a Jew who ate pork all the time. And on Shabbat, he smoked. And he never prayed.

Kahal HaKadosh, I looked at him and I thought, You don't respect the Torah, which is the instruction manual of existence. You don't know it, but you must be less happy than me. I looked at him carefully, and quite honestly, I don't think he lived less well than I do.

So, my friends, if we can be happy without respecting the Torah, why should we exhaust ourselves to apply all these precepts that make life so complicated?

Come on, Abraham, tell us why, we're waiting!

Ha! Ha!

Well, the truth is, I don't know.

Abraham, are you making fun of us, or what?

Are you going to finish your sermon?

What kind of rabbi is this?

A crazy one, that's what!

Come on, let's do the kiddush, because if you're late for dinner your wives will chew me out. Yom hashishi, vaychulu; hashamaayim vehaarets vechol tzevaam...